Assessment and Planning in Health Programs

Assessment and Planning in Health Programs

Bonni C. Hodges, PhD
Associate Professor and Chair
Health Department
State University of New York–Cortland

with

Donna M. Videto, PhD
Associate Professor
Health Department
State University of New York–Cortland

JONES AND BARTLETT PUBLISHERS
Sudbury, Massachusetts
BOSTON   TORONTO   LONDON   SINGAPORE

World Headquarters
Jones and Bartlett Publishers
40 Tall Pine Drive
Sudbury, MA 01776
978-443-5000
info@jbpub.com
health.jbpub.com

Jones and Bartlett Publishers Canada
2406 Nikanna Road
Mississauga, ON L5C 2W6
CANADA

Jones and Bartlett Publishers International
Barb House, Barb Mews
London W6 7PA
UK

Production Credits
Acquisitions Editor: Jacqueline Ann Mark
Senior Production Editor: Julie Champagne Bolduc
Associate Editor: Nicole Quinn
Marketing Manager: Ed McKenna
Director of Interactive Technology: Adam Alboyadjian
Interactive Technology Manager: Dawn Mahon Priest
Manufacturing and Inventory Buyer: Therese Bräuer
Composition: Graphic World
Cover Design: Anda Aquino
Cover Images: (bottom) © AbleStock; (center) © PhotoDisc
Printing and Binding: Malloy, Inc.
Cover Printing: Malloy, Inc.

Library of Congress Cataloging-in-Publication Data
Hodges, Bonni C.
   Assessment and planning in health programs / Bonni C. Hodges, Donna M. Videto.
      p. cm.
   Includes bibliographical references and index.
   ISBN 0-7637-1748-7 (alk. paper)
   1. Health education—Planning. 2. Health promotion—Planning. 3. Health education—Evaluation.
   4. Health promotion—Evaluation. 5. Medical care—Needs assessment.
   [DNLM: 1. Health Education. 2. Program Evaluation—methods. 3. Evaluation Studies. 4. Health
   Promotion. WA 590 H686a 2005] I. Videto, Donna M. II. Title.
   RA440.5.H63 2005
   613—dc21   2004003776

Printed in the United States of America
08 07 06 05 04   10 9 8 7 6 5 4 3 2 1

For Paul, Connor, and Matthew

CONTENTS

Health educators are professionally prepared individuals who take on a variety of roles involving a number of different skills. They are specifically trained to use appropriate educational strategies and methods to facilitate the development of policies, procedures, interventions, and systems that are conducive to the health of individuals, groups, and communities (Gold & Miner, 2002). In other words, they plan, implement, and evaluate programs and interventions that will assist individuals and groups in maintaining and improving their health. The Role Delineation Project conducted during the 1970s and 1980s (Pollack & Carlyon, 1996) determined that there were seven large responsibility areas of the professional health educator.

Assessing individual and community needs for health education is the first of the seven responsibility areas for entry-level health educators listed in *A Competency-Based Framework for Professional Development of Certified Health Education Specialists* (NCHEC, 1996). Planning effective health education programs, implementing health education programs, and evaluating the effectiveness of health education programs are the second, third, and fourth responsibility areas. Each of these responsibility areas contains competencies and subcompetencies that clearly outline what is involved in carrying out each responsibility (Appendix 1). In addition, the Society for Public Health Education (SOPHE) and the American Association for Health Education (AAHE) Joint Committee for Graduate Standards has proposed graduate-level standards that build upon the entry-level framework (Capwell, 1997). Thus, conducting a needs assessment, planning an effective program, implementing programs, and evaluating them are at the core of health education and health promotion.

A Note About Terminology

As you may already know, health education and health promotion are relatively new disciplines that have evolved from other disciplines, such as medicine, public health, sociology, psychology, and political science (Stokols, 1992). Professionals working in these areas have historically used a number of slightly different definitions.

Definitions of health education include the following:

- "The process that bridges the gap between health information and health practices. Health education motivates the person to take the information and do something with it—to keep himself healthier by avoiding actions that are harmful and forming habits that are beneficial" (President's Committee on Health Education, 1973).

- "Any combination of learning experiences designed to facilitate voluntary adaptations of behavior conducive to health" (Green et al., 1980).
- "Any planned combination of learning experiences designed to predispose, enable, and reinforce voluntary behavior conducive to health in individuals, groups, or communities" (Green & Kreuter, 1999).
- "Any combination of planned learning experiences based on sound theories that provide individuals, groups, and communities the opportunity to acquire information and the skills needed to make quality health decisions" (Gold & Miner, 2002).

Definitions of health promotion include the following:

- "The science and art of helping people change their lifestyle to move toward a state of optimal health. Lifestyle is defined broadly, as health promotion programs will not always focus directly on changing health behaviors. Health promotion consists of a balance of physical, emotional, spiritual, intellectual, and social health" (O'Donnell, 1986).
- "Any planned combination of educational, political, regulatory, and organizational supports for actions and conditions of living conducive to health in individuals, groups, or communities" (Green & Kreuter, 1999).

This book will use the 2000 Joint Committee on Health Education and Promotion Terminology document definitions (Gold & Miner, 2002). Every 10 years the AAHE forms a terminology task force, consisting of the Coalition of Health Education Organizations and various health-related federal agencies, to look at current and new terminology in the health education field. The document published by this committee is viewed as the authoritative terminology document for health education terminology, as it standardizes terms, thus, improving communication and understanding among various professions that are associated with health education.

Acknowledgements

We would like to thank the following reviewers:

Jodi Brookins-Fisher, PhD, CHES
Central Michigan University

Georgia Johnston, PhD, CHES
University of Texas, San Antonio

Yasenka Peterson, PhD, CHES
Indiana State University

Jiunn-Jye Sheu, MSPH, PhD, CHES
University of Florida

REFERENCES

Capwell, E. (1997). Health education graduate standards: Expansion of the framework. *Health Education and Behavior, 24*(2), 137–150.

Gold, R. S. & Miner, K. R. (2002). Report of the 2000 Joint Committee on Health Education and Promotion Terminology. *Journal of School Health, 72*(1), 3–7.

Green, L. W. & Kreuter, M. W. (1999). *Health promotion planning: An educational and ecological approach* (3rd ed.). Mountain View, CA: Mayfield.

Green, L., Kreuter, M., Deeds, L. & Partridge, L. (1980). *Health education planning: A diagnostic approach.* Palo Alto, CA: Mayfield.

National Commission for Health Education Credentialling [NCHEC] (1996). *A competency-based framework for professional development of certified health education specialists.* New York: National Commission for Health Education Credentialling.

O'Donnell, M. P. (1986). Definition of health promotion. *American Journal of Health Promotion, 1,* 4–5.

Pollack, M. & Carlyon, W. (1996). The seven responsibilities and how they grew: The story of a curriculum framework. *Journal of School Health, 2,* 291–298.

President's Committee on Health Education (1973). *The report of the President's Committee on Health Education.* Washington, DC: US Government Printing Office.

Stokols, D. (1992). Establishing and maintaining healthy environments: Toward a social ecology of health promotion. *American Psychologist, 47*(1), 6–22.

1

Needs Assessment:
The Big Picture

Key Terms: *APEXPH, community, coalition, health education, health promotion, MAPP, PATCH, needs assessment, Precede–Proceed*

> Dee, a health educator and health education coordinator for a school district, is excited about a new alcohol prevention program that was described at a national conference she recently attended. She implements the program during the new school year. Jose, a health educator with a county health department, had asked the adults on the board of directors at the youth center in his community what health-related programs the youth needed. The board said they thought the youth needed an alcohol prevention program. Jose implements the same program as Dee. After a year, much effort and money, and numerous complaints, neither Dee nor Jose's program is showing positive results. Unfortunately, Dee and Jose did not conduct needs assessments before selecting or implementing their programs.

Perhaps Dee and Jose thought that conducting a needs assessment would be too complicated and time consuming. Maybe they assumed they knew what their target populations needed. Maybe they did not know how to conduct useful needs assessments. However, conducting quality needs assessments would have given them direction in order to target their programs to their specific populations, would have saved their employers time and money, and would have shown that they were health education professionals.

Why Conduct a Needs Assessment?

Dee and Jose are health education professionals, so they know what is "best" with regard to their programs, right? Not exactly. Designing and delivering effective **health promotion** and **health education** programs involve much more than just pulling together a few activities. **Needs assessments** assist the health educator in investigating the web of factors that affect the health of the target population and the ability of health educators to positively influence them. Most of us working in health education and health promotion know and understand that needs assessments can help identify the health problems in the target population, the antecedents to these problems, and corresponding programming needs and ideas. However, needs assessments are also a necessary part of planning and implementing a program and serve as the beginning of program evaluation.

So, more specifically, why do those working in health education and health promotion need to conduct needs assessments before developing and implementing programs?

To Develop a Sense of Connection and Ownership of the Program Among the Target Population

Support for, implementation of, and acceptance of the programs developed will be much stronger and smoother if the target population has been involved in program development. One of the ways to involve the target population is to have members assist in the needs assessment process. Target population members and those closely associated with them can identify sources of needs assessment data, assist in the collection of the data, and provide feedback to program planners regarding the direction of the program. Along the way, target population members begin to see the health problems for themselves, and often become advocates for program areas that they may have resisted if outsiders had merely told them what their problems were. In addition, the target population learns the skills that allow them to periodically update the needs assessments with little or no assistance from professionals. This allows professionals to focus on other areas and empowers the target population, making it more likely that programs will become institutionalized or part of a continuing effort.

Support for and acceptance of programs is more likely when recent data can be provided that paint a picture of the health status of the community or group for which health programming is being designed and can link that picture to needs in the community. A few anecdotes or the impressions of teachers or public safety officers are important but, by themselves, can always be said to just be their biases. An objective, broad presentation of information can unite decision-makers, funding sources, and the target population behind the goal of addressing the greatest health risks in the community. Such a presentation should outline the behaviors, attitudes, and knowledge levels of the target population in various health-related areas; present public health statistics pointing at the most prevalent problems (or those with the greatest incidence); demonstrate where a lack of resources or other barriers are affecting the health of the target population; and provide data about the existing and potential implications of these health problems for the whole community. Many needs assessments also identify the positive assets within the group or community that currently, or could in the future, support health-promoting initiatives. However, it is often most useful to present the health-risk situation first (Bartholomew et al., 2001).

To Provide Information Needed to Seek Resources or Funding

It may be necessary to obtain money or other resources for programs from various groups. Many of these groups require that those seeking funds "prove" the need for funding, materials, or technical assistance. A needs assessment will provide the needed support.

To Identify Barriers and Limitations of a Program You Want to Implement

Needs assessments are integral tools that provide clues to how a new program, or one that is being imported from somewhere else, may have to be planned or adapted to be implemented with a particular targeted group. Comprehensive needs assessments must look beyond information that is exclusive to the group for which the program is intended in order to begin to see potential barriers and limitations to implementing all or part of a planned program.

Although involving the target population in a needs assessment can build support for a program, if key individuals or groups are opposed to the program, it will stand little chance of being implemented as planned or at all, resulting in a waste of time, money, and effort (Basch & Gold, 1986). Thus, collecting information that will identify people and policies that will prevent a program from getting implemented will allow the program planner to develop an acceptable program in an efficient manner. Once the barriers are identified, the program planners can focus on finding ways to remove or modify the barriers in order to continue developing and implementing the program that is supported by other needs assessment data.

Lack of money, time, and trained people to deliver health programs are often other significant barriers (Bartholomew et al., 2001). These should be assessed before planning any program.

To Collect Baseline Data for Evaluation

The evaluation of a program begins with its needs assessment. Data collected during a needs assessment can often serve as part of the baseline or "pretest" data needed for impact and outcome evaluations. This can be attractive to supervisors and funding agencies, because, with proper planning, additional resources will not be needed to collect pretest evaluation data.

To Identify Programming Goals and Objectives

Needs assessments should reveal the health problems in a target population and identify gaps in its wellness levels. Once these areas have been identified, health education and promotion program planners can prioritize the problems and decide which of them should be addressed first. Program goals and program objectives can then be developed to provide direction to program developers. This process results in programming that is developed, implemented, and presented efficiently and that is more likely to be effective in reaching its goals and objectives.

To Achieve the Goals of Our Profession

Sound, efficacious programs and interventions that achieve goals and objectives gain respect for the profession and improve the employment picture. The more successful our programs are and the greater the number of effective programs there are in place, the more opportunities there will be for health educators.

The goal of the needs assessment process is to identify the health needs, educational needs, and resource needs of the target population (Simons-Morton, Greene & Gottleib, 1995). Once identified, program planners can use the information to design health education and health promotion programs that are tailored to their specific groups. Conducting a needs assessment can save money, because a well-targeted program is more likely to be accepted by the target population and become successful, thus saving money on a program that would have had to be abandoned.

Checkpoint 1.1

Look at the definitions of health education and health promotion in the preface. Identify the similarities and differences between them. Which one is broader? Why?

The Role Delineation Project of the 1970s (Pollack & Carlyon, 1996) was the first systematic attempt to define the uniqueness of the professional health educator. Ultimately, it resulted in the recognition of the responsibility areas and competencies that define a health educator. In 1998, the US Department of Labor added health education to its Standard Occupational Classification list and based its definition on the responsibility areas that were previously defined.

The AAHE terminology document defines health educators as those specifically trained to use appropriate educational strategies and methods to facilitate the development of policies, procedures, interventions, and systems conducive to the health of individuals, groups, and communities (Gold & Miner, 2002). Thus, a health educator may conduct health education, health promotion, or both, with individuals or groups, at a number of different sites.

It is useful to think of the health educator as the one primarily responsible for health education and health promotion programs wherever they may occur. So, no matter where or with whom the health educator is working, the responsibilities and competencies of needs assessment, program planning, program implementation, and program evaluation are expected.

> Having decided to conduct needs assessments, Jose and Dee both realize that some review of needs assessment is in order. Jose knows that he has to go out and get some information about alcohol, tobacco, and other drug use in the community but is not sure about how much information he really needs and what data to look for first. He senses that he must be sure to involve health care facilities and worksites in this process. Dee knows from in-class discussions with students that there are some substance use issues among her students. She also knows that she will have to get a broad array of information to conduct a quality needs assessment. However, she has to brush up on the general needs assessment process and on how to collect data.

Conducting a needs assessment entails completing a series of tasks that are repeated with different categories of information in order to clearly identify the priority health-related needs of a well-defined target population. Health educators gather, analyze, and prioritize information across and within groups of similar data to make *systematic, well-informed* decisions regarding the highest and most feasible health-related needs to be addressed with our target population.

The needs assessment begins the process of creating health education and health promotion programs. Once begun, however, it should continue (Figure 1.1).

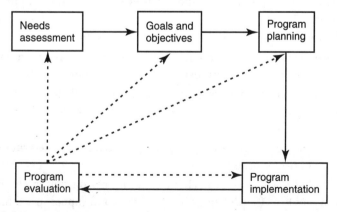

Figure 1.1 Needs assessment, program planning, and evaluation relationship.

Program goals and objectives emerge from the needs assessment process and are used to provide the framework for planning and evaluating programs and interventions. As we reach our goals and objectives, we circle back to the needs assessment to redefine programmatic priorities.

Checkpoint 1.2

List some "communities" other than those determined by geography.

The World Health Organization (WHO) suggests a nine-step framework for conducting a needs assessment (WHO, 2000). These steps provide a useful guide for beginning to plan your needs assessment. The steps are as follows:

1. Decide when to conduct the needs assessment
2. Review available sources of information to decide what information has to be collected and what is already available
3. Decide how to collect the information
4. Develop an action plan that includes cost estimates and approximate time frames
5. Identify and train the assessment team
6. Collect information and data
7. Analyze information and data
8. Interpret analysis to identify priority needs and possible intervention strategies and resources
9. Report on the outcome of the needs assessment to all stakeholders

There are several well-regarded and useful models to assist in mapping your needs assessment process, especially the types of information you will need to collect data (National Academy of Sciences, 2003; Green & Kreuter, 1999; Chapdelaine, n.d.). Basically, all the models provide a slightly different way of saying the same thing:

1. Determine what groups and individuals need to be involved in the needs assessment.
2. Determine readiness and resources for the needs assessment.
3. Involve the target population members in the needs assessment process: actively seek their thoughts, perceptions, and opinions.
4. Find out as much as you can about your target population members' characteristics across a number of different areas related to their lives and their health.
5. Investigate the health status of your target population to determine current health priorities.
6. Find out as much as you can about what may be contributing to the health problems (needs) and what may assist and support in eliminating or decreasing these health problems (assets).

7. Find out as much as you can about why the target population engages in health-risk behaviors.

8. Find out as much as you can about nonbehavioral factors contributing to the health problems and why they exist.

9. Identify people and institutions associated with the target population that act as gatekeepers or agents of change.

10. Be thorough in investigating other programs and interventions and parts of programs and interventions that are attempting to address similar priorities, and find out whether they are working.

In general, as we work through the process, we collect information, analyze the information, select priorities, and then collect more specific information about the priorities. Moving from large to small, we keep narrowing the focus until we have something that the resources and the research can support. Think of it as a series of funnels (Figure 1.2). We then build a program around what is left after the completion of this process.

Planning and conducting a needs assessment can seem like a daunting task. Fortunately, there are models and frameworks to help organize your planning. Brief descriptions of some of the more widely used assessment and planning models are provided here. More detailed descriptions of theses models and frameworks can be found in the profession literature.

Planned Approach to Community Health

The Centers for Disease Control and Prevention (CDC) developed the Planned Approach to Community Health (**PATCH**) in the mid-1980s (USDHHS, n.d.). When we think of **community** as a group of people who have common characteristics such as location, ethnicity, age, or occupation (McKenzie & Smeltzer, 2000), PATCH can be used in a variety of health education and health promotion situations. PATCH provides a general structure for the needs assessment, program planning, and evaluation process that emphasizes community involvement and linkages among a variety of agencies and services associated with the community. PATCH is a general guide consisting of five steps: mobilizing the community; collecting and organizing data; choosing health priorities and target groups; choosing and conducting interventions; and conducting evaluation. The PATCH process guides planners in developing comprehensive health promotion interventions across a variety of settings and situations, including local and state health departments, hospitals, universities, and voluntary agencies (USDHHS, n.d.). The first three of these steps can be considered facets of a needs assessment, but they only serve as a very general reminder of what should be done.

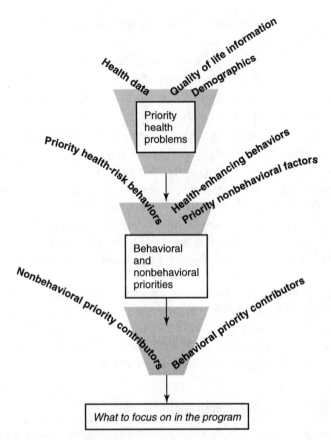

Figure 1.2 Narrow your focus at each step of the needs assessment process.

Review of PATCH-based programs suggests six elements as being critical to successful planning and action in community-based public health programs (National Academy of Sciences, 2003, p. 412). These elements are the existence of a core of community support and participation; data collection and analyses; established objectives and standards to help plan and evaluate; the adoption of multiple strategies in multiple situations; sustained monitoring and progress evaluation to fine-tune programs; and the support of local and national public health agencies.

Assessment Protocol for Excellence in Public Health

The Assessment Protocol for Excellence in Public Health (**APEXPH**) was designed to provide guidance for local health departments in conducting community and organizational self-assessments, planning improvements, and conducting evaluations and reassessments (APHA, n.d.; Chapdelaine, n.d.). It was developed through a cooperative project involving the American Public Health Association (APHA), the Association of Schools of Public Health, the Association of State and Territorial Health Officials, the CDC, and the National Association of City and County Health Officers (NACCHO) and was released in 1991. APEXPH puts the focus on the local health department. The process has three parts.

The first part, *organizational capacity assessment,* directs local health departments to conduct a self-assessment and produce an organizational action plan for correcting perceived weaknesses (APHA, n.d). Those conducting the assessment proceed through six stages: preparing for the organizational capacity assessment; scoring indicators for importance and current status; identifying strengths and weaknesses; analyzing and reporting strengths, analyzing weaknesses; ranking problems in order of priority; developing and implementing action plans; and institutionalizing the assessment process. Areas of self-assessment include, the authority to operate, community relations, community health assessment, financial management, personnel management, program management, policy development, and the assurance of public health services.

The second part, *the community process,* involves the creation of advisory committees of community members that determine the health priorities, set health status goals, and develop program objectives. The advisory committees collect community health data and statistics and community member perception data. The data are reviewed; priorities, goals, and objectives are set; and relevant community resources are identified and mobilized. As in part one, a series of steps are followed: preparing for the community process, collecting and analyzing health data, forming community health committees, identifying community health problems, prioritizing community health problems, analyzing community health problems, creating an inventory of community health resources, and developing a community health action plan.

Part three, *completing the cycle,* involves creating a description of how the organizational action plan and the community health plan are to be monitored and evaluated.

Mobilizing for Action through Planning and Partnership

Mobilizing for Action through Planning and Partnership (**MAPP**) took APEXPH and built upon it to provide a more structured framework for the assessment and program planning process (National Academy of Sciences, 2003). Fundamental to the MAPP process are community organization and partnership development and mobilization to improve quality of life. The MAPP process is centered on four types of assessment that are designed to identify needs and assets associated with fulfilling a shared community vision of quality of life.

MAPP begins by developing partnerships, identifying participants, and then organizing them into workable groups. These groups design the planning process, assess the resources available for MAPP, and determine a management plan for the MAPP process. Those conducting the MAPP program then carry out a process that results in a statement of shared community vision and values. Once the community vision and values statement has been developed, the four MAPP assessments are completed.

The *community themes and strengths assessment* investigates the community's perception of its quality of life and its identification of assets that could be used to improve the health of the community. The *local public health system assessment* is very similar to the organizational capacity assessment of APEXPH and focuses on all of the local organizations that contribute to the health of the community. It answers the questions, what are the components, activities, competencies, and capacities of our local public health system? and how are the essential services being provided to our community? (NACCHO, n.d., p. 1). The *community health status assessment* looks at quality of life and health data in order to determine the health status of the community and to determine priorities for change. The *forces of change assessment* identifies forces and actions external to the public health system that are occurring or might occur and that could affect the health status of the community and the functioning of the local public health system. The four MAPP assessments may be conducted concurrently or sequentially.

The results of the four assessments and the vision and values statements are then used to create a prioritized list of strategic issues. Goals and objectives related to the strategic issues are then developed, before moving into the action cycle. The action cycle consists of planning, implementing, and evaluating programs and activities that will meet the establish goals and objectives.

Precede—Proceed

The Precede portion of the **Precede–Proceed** model (Green & Kreuter, 1999) provides the most comprehensive map of the needs assessment process. It is arguably the most widely used needs assessment model in health education and health promotion, and a large body of literature supports and describes its use (see http://www.ihpr.ubc.ca/precede.html). It helps us by providing a reminder of all the different types of information we should be collecting as part of a needs assessment and by providing a framework for organizing the information, so we can analyze it in a useful manner. Fundamentally, Precede–Proceed acknowledges that health and health behavior result from the interaction of multiple factors and that to have a successful impact on health and health behaviors,

Smaller factors combine to create the health status and quality of life of a population.

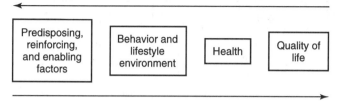

A needs assessment begins by looking at the quality of life and health status, then it identifies the smaller factors that create them.

Figure 1.3 Precede phases for needs assessment.

programs and interventions must be multidimensional. The model is based upon the concept that voluntary behavior change that is supported by the environment is more likely to occur and will last longer than nonvoluntary behavior change. It allows for the consideration and incorporation of health behavior, organizational theories, and social theories into the needs assessment process. Also, it recognizes that when people are involved in determining and prioritizing their own problems and solutions, change is more likely to occur and endure. Essentially, the Precede model cues those working in health education and health promotion to conduct a needs assessment of sufficient breadth to make the success of the eventual program highly likely.

A schematic of Precede–Proceed can be found in Figure 1.3.

The big picture of Precede is that we are working to ultimately improve the quality of life of a group of people. Quality of life is based on many factors, one of which is health. Health is determined by behavioral and lifestyle factors, along with environmental factors. The behaviors and lifestyle result from the existence of and interaction among three categories of factors: predisposing, reinforcing, and enabling. Health promotion and health education programs and activities work to directly affect predisposing, reinforcing, and enabling factors to improve the behavioral and environmental factors contributing to the health problem. When behavioral and environmental factors are more health-enhancing, health status will improve, creating a better quality of life. Proceed reminds us to evaluate the impact of our efforts to implement health promotion and health education programs.

Checkpoint 1.3

Let's say you are working as a school health educator. Which parts of the Precede–Proceed model would you be working with the most? Why? Explain.

The needs assessment framework in Precede–Proceed is considered to be Precede phases 1–4. Figure 1.4 depicts the relationship between the foundations of Precede and its use in needs assessment.

According to Precede we begin our needs assessment by assessing the quality of life of our target population. We do this by collecting statistical and other

Task	Apr	May	Jun	Jul	Aug	Sep	Oct	Nov	Dec	Jan	Feb	Mar
Recruit coalition or advisory board members	X											
First meeting		X										
Establish work groups		X										
Determine needs assessment scope and procedures			X	X								
Develop or acquire materials for data collection				X	X							
Recruit data collectors					X							
Identify and select subjects					X	X						
Train data collectors					X							
Collect data							X	X	X			
Analyze data								X	X			
Make decisions										X		
Validate decisions											X	
Draft report											X	
Final report												X
Write goals and objectives												X

Figure 1.4 Sample timeline for a needs assessment project.

quantitative information, but also by asking members of our target population their perceptions about their quality of life (phase one). We also gather and analyze epidemiologic information about the population (phase two). Using the quality of life information and the epidemiologic information, we determine what the priority health problems are in the target population and select one, and occasionally more, to address. Now, we need to begin to narrow our focus. Phase three involves investigating the behavioral and environmental factors that contribute to the priority health problems we selected in phase two. Again, we analyze our information in order to select behavioral and/or environmental factors that contribute to the existence of the priority health problem. Again, we narrow our focus, gathering information to determine what the predisposing, reinforcing, and enabling factors are that lead to the behavioral and environmental priority factors selected in phase three. We then need to select for change those predisposing, reinforcing, and enabling factors most likely to positively affect the priority behavioral and environmental factors.

The following few chapters will help you learn to conduct a needs assessment by taking you step-by-step through the process. At this point, you may have some questions: What types of information do I need to collect? From whom and how should I collect it? How do I decide upon priorities? How do I begin? Let us get started on answering those questions.

Checkpoint 1.4

Smoking is considered a behavior that contributes to the development of cardiovascular disease (CVD). Brainstorm some factors that contribute to why someone would smoke cigarettes.

Precede can be used in conjunction with other models. For example, Precede can identify specific pieces of information that need to be collected as part of MAPP's four assessments or the community assessment of APEXPH.

Those working in health education and health promotion select needs assessment and program planning models based on the needs of their community and agency or organization, the resources available to conduct the needs assessment, the staff expertise, the available technical support, and the strength and structure of the agency or organization (APHA, n.d.).

The first part of this book is designed to assist you in learning the skills to conduct a solid, valid, useful needs assessment. Subsequent chapters will address how to use the needs assessment to plan health promotion and health education programs and how to evaluate these programs.

Jose and Dee ended up at the same meeting one day and discovered that they were both planning to conduct a needs assessment in the alcohol, tobacco, and other drug area. They have decided to work together and help each other. One of the first actions they took was to call the local university's health department and set up a meeting with one of the faculty who specializes in needs assessments and program planning. They have also begun to discuss when the best time to conduct a needs assessment would be. Dee is thinking that she needs to focus on finding out what the substance use patterns of the youth in the school system are and identifying what factors are contributing to problematic use patterns and groups. She will discuss this with Jose at their next meeting.

Dee and Jose now realize they should have conducted a comprehensive needs assessment before selecting, adapting, and implementing their programs. But how should they begin? It looks like a lot of work, and they both have other responsibilities at their organizations. Besides, money is tight, especially in the health department. Dee now understands that just because she thinks something is a problem, her students and their parents might not (and who knows about the teachers and administrators?). Jose has to deal with the competing interests of the various groups he works with in the community. How will he ever get them to agree on a priority problem?

Organizing Your Needs Assessment

Dee and Jose need to get started, but how? Before they begin to get any information about the needs and assets of their groups, they should do some advanced planning and organizing. Who can help them? How much money and time will they have to conduct their needs assessment? And what tasks will have to be completed before, during, and after the needs assessment? Thinking about and addressing these questions is the first step in the needs assessment process.

Coalitions and Partnerships

Recruiting others to assist in the needs assessment is important. Certainly, including others in the process will keep the workload manageable, but including people and organizations that may be affected by the eventual program can improve the needs assessment, program implementation, program acceptance, and the program itself (NACCHO, n.d.). Coalition and partnership benefits include establishing trust, empowering participants, reducing duplication of services and programs, ensuring accountability, and strengthening social connections and social capital (IOM, 2003).

A **coalition** is formed when groups come together to work toward common goals and objectives (KU Work group, 2000a; CDC, 1995). They are often used in community health promotion planning and implementation. Advisory boards are groups of individuals that represent, at the very least, stakeholders and members of the target population. Advisory boards are common in school buildings and school districts, as well as at worksites and health care facilities. They may also have names such as school council or wellness committee. One could also think of a components of a coordinated school health program as a coalition.

Groups such as these provide assistance with the needs assessment process, facilitate planning, provide or improve communication with the target populations and stakeholders, provide for the consideration of diverse perspectives, and identify potential barriers to program implementation.

A coalition of groups brought together to address common health and health-related problems in a target population can be powerful. There are several important benefits to organizing a coalition for needs assessment and program planning. These include: pooling resources, decreasing unnecessary duplication of efforts, increasing efficiency in program delivery, including and integrating diverse perspectives in the planning process, increasing political clout, improving the ability to gain access to hard-to-reach populations (Wurzbach, 2002; KU Work Group, 2000a; CDC, 1995), and creating greater credibility than an individual institution can have (Wurzbach, 2002).

Building a good coalition takes planning and effort on the part of the agency, institution, or health educator charged with putting one together. Every effort should be made to include a broad array of the target population and organizations and institutions associated with the target population (NACCHO, n.d.). Typically, there is one institution or agency that acts as the lead in putting together and managing the coalition (Wurzbach, 2002). Wurzbach (2002, p. 146) suggests eight steps to building an effective coalition. With regard to a coalition for conducting a needs assessment and planning an intervention, the process of building an effective coalition should include the following:

1. Analyzing the objectives of the coalition to determine whether to form one

2. Recruiting the right people

3. Coming up with a set of preliminary objectives and activities for the coalition, so its members will know what is involved

4. Convening the coalition

5. Anticipating the necessary resources

6. Defining and working toward the elements of a successful coalition for your circumstances

7. Maintaining the viability of the coalition through active management

8. Evaluating the coalition and making improvements where necessary

Common barriers to forming a coalition that works include "turf issues" among groups that perceive themselves as having overlapping missions (KU Work Group, 2000a); previously failed coalitions or other experiences of poor working relationships among groups; dominant individuals, usually professionals, who control discussions and prohibit true participation by the non-professional members of the coalition; lack of funding or lack of flexibility in funding; lack of leadership (KU Work Group, 2000a; CDC, 1995); hidden agendas of some organizations or individual members (CDC, 1995); and potentially complicated decision-making processes (CDC, 1995). The coalition organizer should consider how to address these barriers before assembling the coalition. Establishing clearly communicated procedures for meetings; setting concrete, realistic goals for the coalition; fostering good communication within the coalition; and using inclusive decision-making processes can reduce some of these barriers (KU Work Group, 2000a).

Box 1.1   People and institutions commonly found on health-related coalitions.

Local government representatives	Law enforcement representatives
Health care providers	Local health department employees
YWCA/YMCA	Youth Bureau
Local college and university faculty and staff (departments of health, sociology, and education)	Agency on Aging
	Voluntary agency representatives
United Way	Department of Social Service
Health care administrators	Business owners and managers
Cooperative Extension Employees	Human resources directors
School district faculty and staff	Service organizations (e.g., Rotary or Lions Club)
Target population representatives	Chamber of Commerce

The lead agency, institution, or unit must have the resources necessary to organize and maintain the coalition. If not, the coalition may not work. The lead institution, agency, or unit will be largely responsible for a number of important tasks. Someone from the lead group will need to perform clerical work, such as typing, making phone calls, and photocopying. The lead group facilitates the logistics of coalition meetings by making reminder phone calls, securing meeting locations, providing refreshments, and the like. In addition, it is usually the responsibility of the lead group or individual to coordinate coalition activities and fund-raising (Wurzbach, 2002).

Who is needed on a coalition? The KU Work Group on Health Promotion and Community Development (2000b) identifies several types of people needed on a successful coalition (Box 1.1). Absolutely imperative are stakeholders. These are the people who will be most affected by the work of the coalition. Examples of stakeholders include members of the target population, those responsible for the care of the target population, and the staffs of health care agencies and social service agencies that may be affected by the programs developed by the coalition. Community opinion leaders should also be on your coalition. It is important to identify current emerging leaders.

The initial meetings of the assessment and planning group should focus on organizing the coalition and its process (NACCHO, n.d.). All potential group participants should have a clear idea of the needs assessment project, why they or their groups were invited, estimated time commitments, and expectations for their participation. Subsequent meetings should determine the scope of the needs assessment, establish timelines for completion, and assess available resources. Resources that may be able to be contributed by group members include meeting space, support staff assistance, printing, information gathering, and refreshments.

Coalition Example

The Cortland County (New York) Health Department formed a coalition after receiving a state grant to address CVD in the county (Hodges, Videto & Gefell, 2001). Over 35 groups and individuals were invited to participate in the coalition. Although not all of the invited groups and individuals agreed to participate, the resulting coalition represented a wide spectrum of the county. The health educator in charge of forming the coalition paid special attention to finding groups and indi-

Checkpoint 1.5

You are working for a local branch of the American Cancer Society and want to put together a coalition to address secondary cigarette smoke. Who are some of the people you will ask to be on your coalition?

You are the education director for a community hospital and are setting up an advisory committee in preparation for conducting a needs assessment of the facility's employees. Who will you invite to be on your advisory committee?

viduals to represent areas of the county and constituencies that had traditionally not been included or had not participated in previous health planning initiatives. The recruitment process included telephone contact and letters of invitation. Individuals who had worked with previously underrepresented constituencies were asked to suggest which people from those constituencies should become part of the coalition. The recruitment process included the presentation of county data, showing CVD at higher rates than New York state and the United States; linking the group's mission and constituency to addressing CVD; and making some link to the individual or his or her constituency group and CVD problems. Coalition members chose to participate on one or more initial working groups, which were responsible for data collection, public relations, data analysis, and mini-grant administration. The coalition members were heavily involved in data collection subject identification and access; data collection and public relations logistics; data collection itself, as trained focus group leaders and key informant interviewers; data analysis and interpretation; and priority setting.

The work of the coalition began with a series of monthly meetings. During these early meetings, the group developed a mission statement, broke into workgroups, developed the needs assessment plan, recruited more members to the coalition and the workgroups, and received some training on group process techniques. Meetings were kept to no more than 1.5 hours and included food and attendance incentives, such as t-shirts from current health department programs. After the initial set of meetings, the frequency of the coalition meetings was reduced to once a quarter, usually over lunch, and the work groups became the main avenue of participation for coalition members. Thus, the work groups would meet regularly, usually once a month or more, if needed, and report back to the larger coalition at the quarterly meetings. At the end of the 5-year funding cycle, the coalition had retained 80% of its original members and had added members as the intervention developed. The county health department celebrated the work of this coalition with a luncheon and awards. The school-based intervention that was developed and pilot tested won a statewide award. This coalition secured a second 5-year grant from the state and continues to evolve.

Why was this coalition successful with regard to its ability to work as a group? Table 1.1 suggests why.

Budgets

A budget must be constructed for the needs assessment. In some cases, those in charge of the needs assessment may be told how much money is available to spend, but, in others, they will be asked to request "what you need" as a starting point for determining the funding amount. The first step is to find out how much money the agency or institution has to devote to a needs assessment. The amount of money available will affect decisions you make about how, and how much, information will be collected for the needs assessment. One should also investigate low or no cost resources that may be available. Is there a college or university nearby with faculty or staff who may volunteer for data collection, technical assistance, and other tasks? Does you community have a group of retired citizens that engage in volunteer services? Are there other sources of volunteers? Are there businesses that may donate needed supplies or services? One should also consider seeking grant funds, especially if the estimate of your costs exceeds available resources (HRSA, 2002).

Next, estimate expenses (KU Work Group, 2000b). This can take some detailed thinking. Common expenses are salaries and other personnel costs (e.g., consultant fees), supplies, equipment, telephone costs, and utilities. This estimation may involve researching past records and costs. Be sure to include a miscellaneous category for those expenses that may come up during the needs assessment. It is recommended that you estimate high.

Timelines

Constructing timelines for the general needs assessment process and for specific tasks within the process helps to keep the project on task. The first question here is how much time do we have to do the needs assessment? Once that has been determined, a list of all tasks that must be completed should be made. Those conducting the needs assessment can then determine the timeline and deadlines for completing the tasks (HRSA, 2002).

Table 1.1   Why the Coalition Was Successful

Inclusion of a variety of groups and individuals	Political leaders, school health instructors, a local college health department professor, representatives from all social service and health-related agencies in the county, members of all possible adult and adolescent target populations, and health care workers were included, representing a variety of age groups and income levels.
Clear purpose	The goal was to decrease CVD in the county by addressing physical activity and diet behaviors. The coalition focused largely on environmental and enabling factors.
Active involvement of community agencies	Representatives from all social service and health-related agencies in the county were involved.
Ongoing training for members	Initially training was provided in group process. Additional training was provided as needed for various work groups.
Very active involvement in setting goals and objectives	Coalition members participated in the interpretation of data from needs assessment, selected priorities, and decided on yearly goals and objectives for the coalition and the program.
Productive, well-run meetings	The lead agency provided meeting faciltators. Meetings were efficient, with clear, reasonable agendas, and they were participatory in structure.
Consensus rather than voting	Group processes were used to come to consensus.
Great sense of ownership	High levels of participation in coalition meetings and in a variety of intervention activities, as well as in the institutionalization of many of the original interventions suggest ownership.
Assignment of smaller, manageable pieces	The coalition focused on diet and physical activity risk factors. Work groups were responsible for small chunks of the process or intervention development.
Long-term planning approach	One-year and 5-year work plans were developed.

Based on Wurzbach, M. E. (2002). *Community health education and promotion: A guide to program design and evaluation* (2nd ed.) (pp. 144–161). Gaithersburg, MD: Aspen.

Often, a workplan is developed for specific tasks that must be completed as part of the needs assessment (Table 1.2). Workplans are useful because they specify the necessary tasks, who is responsible for completing the tasks, and the completion deadlines for the tasks.

Dee has decided to create a school district wellness committee, consisting of individuals who represent the eight components of the comprehensive school health model, parents, middle and high school students, and representatives from social service agencies that work with youth—including Jose. Her committee will include district and building representatives. The building representatives will create local building wellness committees. The district committee's first task will be to conduct a needs assessment, in order to update the district's health education curriculum and to identify particular health-related needs of the youth of the county. But before that happens, she will have to work hard at getting people on board and on providing some training to the group on the coordinated school health model and group processing. Dee sees the wellness committee as a "super advisory board."

Jose is happy to have been asked to serve as a coalition member on Dee's wellness committee. However, he realizes that Dee must focus, in some ways, on a broader perspective, while he is responsible for focusing on substance use and abuse in the county. Thus, he has begun to brainstorm and list people and organizations that are involved in substance use issues. Perhaps a coalition could serve to pool everyone's resources and prompt them to move forward with some new initiatives—the first being a comprehensive needs assessment in the substance use and abuse area.

Summary

Needs assessment entails a series of data collection, data analysis, and priority setting tasks, which are designed to provide the foundation for developing and implementing a meaningful program. Engaging in needs assessment activities not only helps to identify goals and objectives but develops connections with target populations and stakeholders, provides information necessary to seeking funding, defines the parameters of the program, and provides baseline evaluation data. A systematic plan for conducting a needs assessment should be developed. Models such as Precede–Proceed, APEXPH, and MAPP can be used to develop needs assessment plans.

Table 1.2 Sample Work Plan for Conducting Focus Groups

Activities	Responsible Party	Timeline	Resources required
Obtain permission to conduct focus groups.	Health coordinator	January	
Develop or adapt focus group questions.	Health coordinator Focus group work group	February–March	Focus group guides from similar needs assessments
Select focus group participants.	Health coordinator Health teachers Students	March	Student enrollment lists from all schools participating
Select and train focus group moderators and observers.	Health coordinator Consultant from the college	March	Video camera, monitors, tapes Audio cassette tapes and players Snacks
Secure appropriate space to conduct focus groups.	Health coordinator	March	
Conduct focus groups.	Trained focus group moderators and observers	April	Video camera, monitors, tapes Audio cassette tapes and players Snacks Gift card incentives
Analyze and interpret focus group data.	Focus group work group Consultant from the college	May–June	Qualitative data analysis software
Write a focus group report.	Focus group work group	July	

QUESTIONS

1. Why is it important to conduct needs assessments?
2. How are needs assessment, program planning, and evaluation related?
3. What are MAPP, APEXPH, and PATCH? How are they used?
4. In general, what are the basic steps of a needs assessment?
5. Define health education, health educator, and health promotion.

EXERCISES

1. Go to the professional journals. Locate and read one article describing a health promotion program and one describing a health education program. Write a short paper describing the similarities and differences between the types of activities that were undertaken in the programs you read about.

2. Find out when the next certified health education specialist (CHES) exam is offered, and where the nearest testing site is. Interview a professional who has the CHES credential. Find out why this person became a CHES and what benefits this person gets from this title.

3. Locate and read an article from a professional journal that explains the application of the Precede portion of the Precede–Proceed model, PATCH, APEXPH, or MAPP. Write a summary and share it with your class.

4. Go to http://mapp.naccho.org/mapp_introduction2.asp. Select one of the MAPP phases. Read about the phase and look at the worksheets that are available on the Web site. Write a two-page summary of the phase, and bring it to class to share. Be able to describe for the class the types of worksheets that are available on the Web site.

5. Contact a local health department, worksite wellness program, health care organization, voluntary organization, or health education curriculum director. What planning models have they used in the past? Why did they use them?

6. Locate some professional literature on CVD, its causes, and its effects on quality of life. Put the causes and effects in the appropriate place using the Precede model.

7. Locate some professional literature on the factors that contribute to smoking cigarettes. List the factors that you find. Can you group factors

that are similar into two or more groups? Explain the similarities of the factors in each of your groups.

REFERENCES

American Public Health Association [APHA] (n.d.). *The guide to implementing model standards.* Retrieved August 9, 2003, from http://www.apha.org/ppp/science/theguide.htm.

Bartholomew, L. K., Parcel, G. S., Kok, G. & Gottleib, N. H. (2001). *Intervention mapping: Designing theory- and evidence-based health promotion programs.* Mountain View, CA: Mayfield.

Basch, C. E. & Gold, R. S. (1986). The dubious effects of type V errors in hypothesis testing on health education practice and theory. *Health Education Research, 1*(4), 299–305.

Centers for Disease Control and Prevention [CDC] (1995). *Guidelines for health education and risk reduction activities.* Atlanta, GA: Centers for Disease Control and Prevention.

Chapdelaine, P. A. (n.d.). PATCH/APEXPH: *Community health planning, summary of two models.* Nashville, TN: Meharry Medical College. Retrieved August 9, 2003, from http://www.naturalhealthbridge.com/msph/msphpatch.htm.

Gold, R. S. & Miner, K. R. (2002). Report of the 2000 Joint Committee on Health Education and Promotion Terminology. *Journal of School Health, 72*(1), 3–7.

Green, L. W. & Kreuter, M. W. (1999). *Health promotion planning: An educational and ecological approach* (3rd ed.). Mountain View, CA: Mayfield.

Health Resources and Services Administration [HRSA] (2002). *Ryan White CARE act needs assessment guide.* Washington, DC: US Department of Health and Human Services.

Hodges, B. C., Videto, D. M. & Gefell, T. (2001). *Moving marathon: The success of a healthy heart coalition.* Paper presented at the SOPHE Annual Meeting in Atlanta, GA.

Institute of Medicine [IOM] (2003). *The future of the public's health.* Washington, DC: National Academies Press.

KU Work Group on Health Promotion and Community Development (2000a). Chapter 5, Section 5: Coalition building I: Starting a coalition. Lawrence, KS: University of Kansas. Retrieved January 30, 2003, from http://ctb.ukans.edu/tools/EN/sub_section_main_1057.htm.

KU Work Group on Health Promotion and Community Development (2000b). *Community tool box.* Lawrence, KS: University of Kansas. Retrieved January 30, 2003, from http://ctb.lsi.ukans.edu/tools/EN/sub_section_main_1303.htm.

McKenzie, J. F. & Smeltzer, J. L. (2000). *Planning, implementing, and evaluating health promotion programs: A primer* (3rd ed.). Boston: Allyn & Bacon.

National Academy of Sciences (2003). *The future of public health in the 21st century.* Washington, DC: National Academies Press.

National Association of County and City Health Officials [NACCHO] (n.d.). *Mobilizing for action through planning and partnerships.* Retrieved July 15, 2003, from http://mapp.naccho.org/MAPPModel.asp.

Pollack, M. & Carlyon, W. (1996). The seven responsibilities and how they grew: The story of a curriculum framework. *Journal of School Health, 2,* 291–298.

Simons-Morton, B., Green, L. & Gottleib, N. (1995). *Introduction to health education and health promotion* (2nd ed.). Prospect Heights, IL: Waveland.

US Department of Health and Human Services [USDHHS] (n.d.). *Planned approach to community health: Guide for the local coordinator.* Atlanta, GA: US Department of Health and Human Services; Centers for Disease Control and Prevention; National Center for Chronic Disease Prevention and Health Promotion. Retrieved February 1, 2003, from http://www.cdc.gov/nccdphp/patch.

World Health Organization [WHO] (2000). *Reproductive health during conflict and displacement: A guide for programme managers.* Geneva, Switzerland: World Health Organization. Retrieved November 13, 2002, from http://www.who.int/reproductivehealth/publications/RHR_00_13_RH_conflict_and_displacement/PDF _RHR_00_13/chapter10.en.pdf.

Wurzbach, M.E. (2002). *Community health education and promotion: A guide to program design and evaluation* (2nd ed.) (pp. 144–161). Gaithersburg, MD: Aspen.

2

Paint a Picture of Your Target Population: Assessing Assets and Problems

Key Terms: *quality of life, community capacity, morbidity, mortality, incidence, prevalence, predisposing factor, reinforcing factor, enabling factor, resources*

Dee's wellness committee has decided that it would like to take a look at the "big picture" of health in the community before it makes any decisions about what the school health program needs to address. The local health department representative on the committee thinks this is a great idea and offers to coordinate a review of the community's quality of life and health status. He has even offered to contribute some funds to the effort, because his office can use the information for its own planning. Jose agrees to assist with this effort, because his coalition may also benefit from the data that are gathered. Jose and the health department representative organize a work group to conduct this portion of the needs assessment. Two other members of the wellness committee join them and agree to recruit community members. They set up a meeting and agree to generate a set of questions that they think this portion of the needs assessment should answer.

Planning a program begins with a comprehensive needs assessment. The needs assessment allows program planners to "paint a picture" of the target population in order to decide what the program should address, how to go about addressing it, and who should be involved. In essence, a needs assessment consists of a number of stages of increasingly narrow focus. Within each stage, data are collected, organized, and analyzed in order to determine the priority factors that the subsequent stage then investigates. At the end of the needs assessment process program, there remains a set of concrete, supportable, measurable factors that are connected to one or more health priorities of the target population. These are the factors that program planners will address in the program that is eventually developed.

This chapter outlines the stages of a needs assessment for health education and a health program, focusing on the types of information that are necessary to consider within each stage. Data collection techniques are referred to in this chapter but are discussed in more detail in Chapter 7.

Quality of Life and Health Status Assessment

Clark (2000) argues that, in the 21st century, health-related professionals will increase their focus and acceptance of quality of life as the goal of health programs and interventions. Green and Kreuter (1999) emphasize the need for all to understand the reciprocal nature of health and social issues. Bartholomew and colleagues (2001) point out the importance of assessing the target community's or population's abilities and current and future resources; together, these are often referred to as **community capacity** (CDC, 1997). Thus, a comprehensive needs assessment begins by looking at a group's quality of life (NACCHO, n.d.; Green & Kreuter, 1999).

The health status of a group of people is really one part of its overall quality of life. Yet, because health educators are most interested in health, we need to be sure to make a detailed assessment of health status that is separate from an assessment of quality of life. Being able to link health problems and priorities to deficits in quality of life strengthens any argument for their need to be addressed and is the ultimate goal of health interventions (Clark, 2000; Green & Kreuter, 1999). The identification of a community's capacity and strengths (Box 2.1) can point towards intervention strategies that may be more successful or resources that can be used to address health problems (Bartholomew et al., 2001; NACCHO, n.d.). One should keep in mind two points about the notion of community. First, communities are not just geographically bound; they may comprise a group of people with shared interests, goals, and backgrounds. Second, the schools, worksites, health care facilities, and other smaller groups with which we may work or be responsible for exist in a larger geographic community and may be affected by the assets and problems of the larger community.

What is **quality of life**? What information are we looking to gather when we do what Green and Kreuter (1999) call a social assessment? Quality of life is the sense of individuals and groups of having their needs met and being free from barriers to opportunities to become happy and fulfilled (Green & Kreuter, 1999); it describes how "good" their lives are (Raphael, Steinmetz & Renwick, 1998). But what makes a good life? Raphael, Steinmetz, and Renwick (1998)

Box 2.1 What is community capacity?

Together and separately, individuals in a community have particular strengths and skills that, now and in the future, may contribute to the quality of life of the entire community.* This is community capacity. Assessing and identifying community capacity should be part of a comprehensive health needs assessment. Community capacity building may need to be an early part of any health-related intervention. But what should be measured? The Vancouver Health Authority in Vancouver, Canada, identified five dimensions of community capacity. When applied to health, these can be thought of as follows:

1. Skills and knowledge needed for the effective planning and delivery of programs
2. Leadership that allows for the organization of the talent and skills present in the community to collectively address a health issue or problem
3. A sense of confidence within the community that it can effectively address its health-related problems
4. Existing social capital, trust, and connectedness within the community that will allow for collective health problem-solving
5. A cultural environment that supports the learning and consideration of new ideas and the trial of new approaches

*Centers for Disease Control and Prevention; Agency for Toxic Substances and Disease Registry, Committee on Community Engagement (1997). *Principles of community engagement.* Atlanta, GA: Public Health Practice Program Office. Retrieved April 1, 2003, from http://www.cdc.gov/phppo/pce/index.htm; Vancouver Coastal Health Authority (n.d.). *Community and public involvement.* Retrieved April 1, 2003, from http//www.vcn.bc.ca/vrhb/SMCHTF/CommunityCapacity/CommunityCapacity.htm.

---

discuss three elements of quality of life: being, belonging, and becoming. Essentially, having a good life consists of having a combination of these three elements. It involves being psychologically, physically, and spiritually healthy and being able to be autonomous (being); feeling as if one is connected to other individuals, community resources and services, and the surrounding physical environment (belonging); and having available and engaging services and activities (in leisure time, education, or work) to achieve fulfillment and happiness (becoming).

Collecting existing information about various aspects of the community or group and finding out what the perceptions of the community or group members are regarding their individual and community quality of life allows one to paint a picture of the quality of life and health status of the target group. Locating, compiling, and organizing existing data through document reviews is part of this process (Green & Kreuter, 1999). Primary data collection is used to measure perceptions of the target group members and stakeholders about quality of life and social needs. It is also used to measure assets.

Listening to the target population members and engaging them in these tasks whenever possible is a vital.

Painting the picture of your group's quality of life begins with reviewing its demographic information (Hodges, 1997). Population numbers and characteristics are easily attainable from US Census data and other state and local agencies, such as the Chamber of Commerce, local government offices, and local departments of labor. Gender, racial and ethnic characteristics, income levels, and education levels should also be obtained. It is useful to look at how these characteristics, and perhaps others, are distributed across your target population. For example, are some areas of the community wealthier and better educated levels than other areas? Are there clusters of cultural groups? This information may become important later on in the process when selecting priorities and developing interventions.

In order to build a community profile of assets and capacity, the existence of and participation in civic, cultural, religious, and social service organizations should be documented (Minkler & Wallerstein, 1997). The number and types of local financial organizations, child care organizations, hospitals, institutions of higher education, small and large businesses, public schools, libraries, voluntary and social organizations, and communications and media organizations should be noted. Community members' participation in and interactions with these organizations should also be noted. These organizations can be identified by looking in local telephone books, reading the classified and other advertisements in the local papers, contacting the Chamber of Commerce and other local organizations associated with institutions of interest, and asking community members. Compiling information about the amounts and locations of green space, the variety and conditions of housing, the availability of health resources, and the capacity and skills of the community will contribute to your picture. Gathering crime statistics, school and work absenteeism rates, discrimination levels, unemployment rates, voting rates, public assistance rates, and measures of crowding will also help to assess quality of life (Green & Kreuter, 1999). Taking windshield tours, reading local newspapers and online publications, reviewing existing documents, and conducting key informant and other types of interviews are often included in compiling this information.

Coalition members, advisory groups, and their community representatives will be helpful in identifying documents to review, describing how to locate and access the documents, identifying subgroups to include in the process as sources of information, and securing access and permission to collect data from hard-to-reach groups. Some common sources of secondary data and primary data collection methods for this portion of the needs assessment are discussed subsequently. However, keep in mind that a thorough review of the professional literature will reveal and suggest data collection strategies that may be more specific to your situation.

Box 2.2 provides suggestions for questions to form the basis of a quality of life primary assessment (Raphael, Steinmetz & Renwick, 1998). These questions have been used in focus groups, individual interviews, and community forums.

Box 2.2 Suggested questions for a primary quality of life assessment.

For Community Members:

What is it about your neighborhood and community that makes life less than good for you and the people you care about?

What are some of the things in your neighborhood and community that help you and your family cope or manage when you or your family have problems?

What would you like to see added to your neighborhood or community that would help you cope or manage when you have problems? Are there services you would like to see? What programs would you like to see?

For Service Providers:

What is it about this neighborhood or community that makes life good for people who live here?

What are some of the problems that exist for people who live in this community?

How do these issues relate to the mandate or mission of your agency?

How does your agency attempt to improve the quality of life of community members?

Can you give some examples of things your agency is doing that are working well? What is not working so well?

What are some barriers that keep your agency from carrying out these efforts? What helps you carry out your efforts?

For Elected Officials:

What is it about this neighborhood or community that makes life good for people who live here?

What are some of the problems that exist for people who live in this community?

How do these issues relate to your role as an elected representative?

How do you attempt to improve the quality of life of community members?

Can you give some examples of things you have done for the community that have been successful? What has been unsuccessful?

What are some barriers that keep you from carrying out these efforts? What helps you carry out these efforts?

Source: Adapted from Raphael, D., Steinmetz, B. & Renwick, R. (1998). *How to carry out a community quality of life project: A manual.* Toronto, Canada: University of Toronto.

As you can see, these questions ask respondents to discuss what is good and not so good about their community and to identify any needs that could help improve the quality of life. These can be easily adapted for needs assessment use in worksite, school, health care facilities, and other sites. Responses from these questions can then be looked at from the perspective of being, belonging, and becoming to make a determination about community members' perceptions of their quality of life. These questions, or others like them that are developed by your assessment planning group, can be used in the context of key informant interviews, focus groups, community forums, and surveys. In addition, photo novella/photo voice is a particularly good technique to use to foster target group participation and to include a wide variety of perspectives (Wang, 2003). Photo novella/photo voice is discussed in more detail in Chapter 7.

Document review will provide much of the other necessary data for the quality of life assessment. The planning group will need to determine what data is necessary, where it is located, and how to access and record

Checkpoint 2.1

You want to do a quality of life assessment on your campus. What types of data are you going to collect?

Indicator	Current local data	Current state data	Current national data	Healthy People 2010 goal				
Registered voters who voted in last election				NA				
Children receiving public assistance (%)				NA				
Child care slots								
Mortality rates								
	Female	Male	Female	Male	Female	Male	Female	Male
Coronary heart disease								
Lung cancer								
Stroke/CVA								
Incidence rates								
Coronary heart disease								
Lung cancer								
Stroke/cerebrovascular accident (CVA)								

Figure 2.1 Example of a health data recording sheet. The type of rate (e.g., rate per 10,000) and the year represented by the data should be recorded.

it. A systematic method to record and present your secondary data should be developed, such as is shown in Figure 2.1.

Health Status Assessment

What is the health status of your target population? Which health problems affect the most people? Which ones are on the rise? Which ones are decreasing in incidence and prevalence? How does your target population compare to state and national rates on various health problems? Is it healthier, on par, or worse? What health problems does your target population think are important to change? Do health problems appear at different rates among subgroups within your target population? On what health problems does your agency's or employer's funding source focus? Do your health data identify problems that have been selected as priorities in Healthy People 2010 (USDHHS, 2000) or a comparable state or regional document? What health problems may be having a direct impact on quality of life issues?

These are the major questions that the health status assessment portion of the needs assessment seeks to answer. They may appear to be easy questions to answer, and they often are. However, the challenge of the health assessment is for the planning group to consider the answers to all these questions, along with the quality of life information, in order to identify priority health problems.

In many situations, the focus of the health assessment will be limited or defined by employers or funding sources. Health care agencies and organizations may only want to focus on particular types of health problems in a community, mandated curriculum areas of a school, or a narrow range of health problems at a worksite. For example, in New York, local health departments compete for "healthy heart" grant monies that are given out by the New York State Department of Health (NYSDOH) (2000). Part of the grant application includes painting a picture of the "heart health" of the population served by the local health department. For those working on these projects, all data in the health assessment relate to the various CVDs. Once awarded the grant, the local departments have to revisit their health assessment information, perhaps adding to it, in order to more clearly define the health priorities to be addressed by the programs that will be developed.

Several types of epidemiologic data must to be collected in order to assess health status (NACCHO, n.d.; Green & Kreuter, 1999; CDC, 1992). These data assist in the priority selection process by providing information about the existence of actual and potential health problems (CDC, 1992). These data identify where health problems are; who is at risk; and which problems are, or have the potential to be, increasing or decreasing. These include **morbidity, mortality**, disability, **incidence**, **prevalence**, distribution, and trends across recent time frames. These data should be collected for the target population and at least one comparison population. Comparison populations can be groups similar to the target population, the state population that is home to the target population, or the population of entire country. It is also important to collect the health data by subgroup (e.g., gender, racial or ethnic group, and geographic group) when available, as this may help to pinpoint specific targets of intervention. Incidence rates highlight new cases of a health problem in a population (CDC, 1992). They are the most common means to measure and compare the frequency of a health problem in a population. The higher the incidence rate, the greater the problem. Prevalence rates look at *all* the cases of a health problem in a population, new and old. Years of potential life lost (YPLL) rates look at premature death in a given population from specific health problems.

Box 2.3   Common epidemiology terms for needs assessments.*

Morbidity rates describe the existence of or probability of occurrence of a health problem in a population.

Incidence rate:

$$\frac{\text{The number of new cases of a specific health problem reported during a given time frame} \times 10^n}{\text{Average population during the given time frame}}$$

Point prevalence rate:

$$\frac{\text{The number of (current new + old) cases of a specific health problem at a given point in time} \times 10^n}{\text{Estimated population at the same point in time}}$$

Period prevalence rate:

$$\frac{\text{The number of current (new + old) cases of a specific health problem over a given period of time} \times 10^n}{\text{Estimated population at midpoint of the given time frame}}$$

Mortality rates describe deaths in a population.

Crude:

$$\frac{\text{Deaths during a given time frame} \times 10^n}{\text{Size of the population among which the deaths occurred}}$$

Cause specific:

$$\frac{\text{Deaths from a specific cause} \times 10^5}{\text{Population at midpoint of the given time frame}}$$

*Centers for Disease Control and Prevention [CDC] (1992). *Principles of epidemiology* (2nd ed.). Atlanta, GA: Centers for Disease Control and Prevention, Public Health Practice Program Office.

A review of epidemiology is beyond the scope of this text; however, a brief review of those terms important for needs assessment can be found in Box 2.3.

Epidemiologic data for reportable conditions are relatively easy to locate; although, it should be kept in mind that all reportable cases may not be communicated to local health departments (CDC, 1992). The CDC, through publications such as the *Morbidity and Mortality Weekly Report* (MMWR), the National Center for Health Statistics, and state and local health departments have a vast array of health status data available for use. Many voluntary agencies, such as the American Cancer Society and the American Heart Association, may also have some useful health status data. The challenge is to locate data that are most specific to your target population.

What the target population thinks are priority health problems must also be assessed and included in setting health priorities (NACCHO, n.d.). The target population and stakeholders should be asked what the health problems are as part of the primary data collection activities that concern quality of life or health status. Epidemiologic data may also be presented to community members and groups for comment, feedback, and participation in setting health priorities. Often, both strategies are employed. Key informant interviews, focus groups, community forums, and surveys can be used to obtain perceptions of health priorities.

Checkpoint 2.2

You are working in the infectious disease branch of a local health department. You need to do a health assessment. Identify three federal sources of epidemiologic data that would be appropriate to use to compare to your local data.

Selecting Health Priorities

As mentioned previously, the selection of health priorities includes consideration of the quality of life assets and needs and the health data that were collected. Those involved in the process look at all the information in order to identify gaps between where the target group is and where it wants and needs to be with regard to health and quality of life. First, the data are organized and presented to those involved in the decision-making process. The data then are reviewed and considered in a systematic fashion in order to arrive at a list of health priorities. These priorities are then presented to the target population for feedback and validation and are adjusted as needed. Let us explore this in more detail.

The data that were collected should be organized and presented in ways that make the data easy to use and understand for those involved in the setting of priorities. Charts, graphs, summary tables, and other visual depictions of the data collected should be prepared for use in the decision-making process (NACCHO, n.d.).

The target population and the stakeholders must be involved in the selection of priorities. This may be accomplished through a coalition structure, by having community forums or other open communication methods, or by setting up ad hoc committees or working groups. Often, some form of systematic group process, such as a nominal group process, is used. Community-based participatory research (CBPR), which is growing in use and favor in health education and health promotion takes the position that community members should participate equally with experts in all steps of the needs assessment process and decision-making process (Minkler & Wallerstein, 2003).

What should be considered when making a decision about health priorities? Part of the decision-making process involves looking at how the target population data compares to the comparison population data that were collected. For example, let us say you are working for the American Cancer Society. Your data suggest that the breast cancer and the lung cancer mortality and prevalence rates for your region are comparable and higher than other cancer rates. Upon further review of the data, it is apparent that the state and national prevalence rates for lung cancer for the group were higher than both the state and national overall rates for the past 3 years. Furthermore, the breast cancer rate was lower than either the state or national rates. With this information, it is likely that many would consider lung cancer to be a bigger priority than breast cancer. However, it is often not that simple. The decision-makers must look at all the data. Considering how trend data compare is also helpful. Have the breast and lung cancer rates been increasing or decreasing in the region? How do the trend data compare to the state or nation?

How the health problems are related to quality of life issues must also be considered during priority selection. Are there any direct or indirect links? For example, are high asthma hospitalization rates contributing to school absenteeism rates? Are Medicare and Medicaid expenditures disproportionately high for particular conditions that are apparent in the community health data? Those health problems that can be linked to factors that have a negative impact on quality of life should be considered as priorities.

Other questions to consider during this process are as follows (NACCHO, n.d.):

- What are the perceptions of the target population and the stakeholders, and how do they compare to the other data that were collected?
- Are there disproportionate rates of health problems in certain subpopulations?
- What existing resources are available to address a problem?
- Does the community, agency, organization, school, or worksite have the capacity to address the problem?
- What are the consequences of not addressing the problem?

It is important to communicate the collected data and, when determined, the initial priorities to the target population and the community at large for validation, comment, and eventual acceptance (NACCHO, n.d.). Adjustments to the initial health priorities can be made based on the feedback.

To some, conducting a quality of life assessment and a health assessment may seem unnecessary or a waste of time. Let us say you work for the American Cancer Society, you are a school health educator with a set curriculum, or you are a worksite wellness coordinator who is only concerned with the employees at your site. Why should the planning group take the time to look at quality of life or consider a variety of health problems? First of all, it is useful to validate and update what you already know. Which type of cancer is currently the biggest problem for your target group, or do different subgroups have different cancer priorities? What are the current or growing health problems in the community and school-age populations, and does your school health curriculum give sufficient attention to them and their causes? Are their health problems in the greater community that can impact the employees?

The answers to these questions can help develop a program that is relevant to the target group. It is also important to find out if the perceptions of the target group and stakeholders are in line with the epidemiologic data. If this is not done, planners may develop a program that the target group and the stakeholders think is unnecessary, negatively impacting its success. Conducting the quality of life and health status assessment can also serve to motivate the stakeholders and the target population and contribute to the acceptance of the interventions that are developed. An investigation of quality of life, community or group capacity, and assets will assist the program planner in these situations in developing a program that is more relevant to the target group than one that would result without the additional data (Box 2.4).

The health assessment process, together with the quality of life assessment, identifies those health problems that need to be addressed in the immediate future. Once determined, the subsequent parts of the needs assessment will attempt to explain why the priority health problems exist so that program planners can design interventions to improve the health status of the target population.

Jose's work group members put together a grid that identified each question they wanted to get answered, three potential secondary sources of information to answer each question, and a person responsible for getting the information. They would have liked to have conducted focus groups to collect some data about community member perceptions of quality of life, but they did not have the time or the funding. Instead, they conducted several key informant interviews. They reconvened after 6 weeks to share what they had collected. In order to assist with the priority setting, they constructed a chart that included

---

Box 2.4   The coordinated school health model and quality of life assessment.

It is useful and informative to conduct a quality of life assessment of a community in which a particular school or school district exists; however, in many cases, the school health educator may want to look specifically at the quality of life within the school or its district. From the perspective of the coordinated school health model, we would want to also get perceptions of faculty and staff, students, and parents about being, belonging, and becoming within the school or district. The CDC's *School Health Index* materials (available to download from http://www.cdc.gov/nccdphp/dash)* and the Mariner Model Assessment† both provide a good basis for taking a look at the quality of life in schools from the coordinated school health perspective. Those working on particular worksites may also wish to assess the quality of the work environment for its employees.

---

*Centers for Disease Control and Prevention (2000). *School health index for physical activity and healthy eating: A self-assessment and planning guide* (Elementary school version). Atlanta, GA: Centers for Disease Control and Prevention.
† Hoyle, T. (1996). *The Mariner model: Charting the course for health-promoting schools and communities.* Summerville, SC: Hoyle and Associates.

---

pieces of information for the local area, comparison information, and state and local objectives. At this meeting, the group decided that it will conduct several focus groups and at least three community forums, run by the neighborhood associations, to get feedback from community members about the information the group has collected. Jose will also write a piece for the local paper, outlining the community assets that were revealed as part of this process. Once the work group receives feedback from the community, it will conduct a group processing activity with the coalition to select health priorities.

Determining the Sources of Priority Health Problems

The coalition has determined that lung cancer, chronic obstructive pulmonary disease, and other respiratory problems are the highest priorities in the community. "Cigarette smoking!" exclaimed the coalition. However, Jose and Dee know that it is not that simple and that they need to take a more comprehensive look at what the contributors to the respiratory problems may be.

You have determined one or more priority health problems. But how do you combat the problem? What needs to be changed? The next step in the needs assessment process is to figure out what factors are contributing to the development of this health problem and to select those factors that your program will focus on improving or fostering in order to improve the health problem. These should be factors that directly contribute to the problem. A thorough review of the professional journals and other professional documents, such as health-related government documents, voluntary agency reports, and consensus reports from organizations that fund or publish health-related scientific research (e.g., Institute of Medicine and Carnegie Council for Adolescent Development), should be conducted. A comprehensive list, including both individual and group factors, should be developed (Green & Kreuter, 1999). See Table 2.1 for a list of factors that might be developed to explain West Nile virus (CDC, n.d.a).

Once the list of factors has been made, it is useful to group them as behavioral or environmental (NACCHO, n.d.; Green & Kreuter, 1999). Green and Kreuter (1999) suggest an additional group of nonchangeable factors. Nonchangeable factors are those such as age, gender, climate, physical and mental impairments, and existing disease states. Although not amenable to change through health promotion or health education, these factors should be taken into account when determining targets for the intervention activities. Behavioral factors are those actions that promote health, prevent a specific health problem, promote self-care, and control the development of more serious complications. Individual and collective behaviors may directly contribute to the health problem or indirectly contribute through their effects on environmental factors (Figure 2.2). Environmental factors include both social and physical factors, such as social norms and living conditions, respectively.

Table 2.1	**Factors Contributing to West Nile Virus**

Not applying insect repellent containing DEET

Climate that is conducive to mosquito breeding

Geographic area that contains water for mosquito breeding

Not wearing appropriate protective clothing

Being outside at peak mosquito biting times (dawn and dusk)

Not wearing long pants, long sleeves, and socks when outdoors

Using insect repellent inappropriately

No local mosquito control program

Lots of locations for standing water to accumulate

Not eliminating items and places that could hold standing water

Not emptying standing water sites

Source: Centers for Disease Control and Prevention, Division of Vector-Borne Infectious Diseases (n.d.). *West Nile virus basics—Prevention: Avoid mosquito bites to avoid infection.* Retrieved April 5, 2003, from http://www.cdc.gov/ncidod/dvbid/westnile/index.htm.

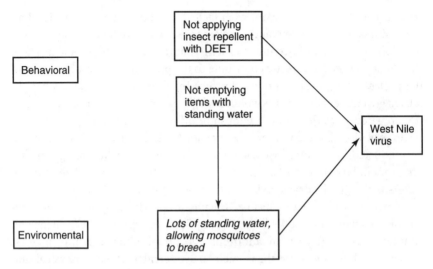

Figure 2.2 Example of the relationship between behavioral and environmental factors for West Nile virus.

Environmental factors may contribute to the health problem directly or through their effects on behavior.

Once a list of factors, categorized into groups, has been established the following must be determined: Which of the behavioral and environmental factors are present in the target population or community? To what degree are they present? What does the target population consider to be contributing to the health problem? As with the quality of life and the health assessment, begin by looking for existing data for the target group or community. Have others recently measured the prevalence of behavioral and environmental factors in the group of interest? The coalition and advisory group will help in identifying what data may have already been collected and where this data can be found. The local United Way, local and regional voluntary organizations, school districts, agencies on aging, employee assistance programs, and the like may have recently collected data for their own purposes. Perhaps behavioral and environmental data were already collected and presented in existing documents that were reviewed earlier in the process. If so, revisit those documents. As you identify existing data, pay attention to how recent the data are, the similarity of the groups from which they were collected to your group, and whether proper data collection techniques were used (Melnick, 2000).

The initial list of factors is then reviewed, guided by the following questions: Can any of the behaviors be grouped together based on who engages in

Checkpoint 2.3

Identify three agencies, government organizations, or ongoing surveillance studies that could provide you with behavioral and environmental factors that contribute to respiratory diseases.

them, or can any of the environmental factors be grouped together by who can effect change in them (e.g., individuals at risk, health care providers, and politicians)? Can any of the behaviors be grouped together because they are part of a larger behavior? Do any of the behaviors need to be broken down into smaller behaviors?

Let us return to the list of factors related to West Nile virus. The behaviors in this list include: not applying insect repellent containing DEET; not wearing long pants, long sleeves, and socks when outdoors; being outside at dawn or dusk; not wearing appropriate protective clothing; and not emptying standing water sites. Reviewing this list, one could devise the groupings shown in Table 2.2.

Take a look at the behavioral factors more closely. First, we can see both "not wearing appropriate protective clothing" and "not wearing long pants, long sleeves, and socks when outdoors." The second factor more specifically indicates what is meant by "wearing appropriate protective clothing." This is a much better statement of the behavioral factor than "not wearing protective clothing" and is potentially more measurable. Second, we see "using insect repellent inappropriately." This may be an important factor, but we need to further break this behavior down. What is inappropriate use? We must go back to our professional sources to further delineate the behavior of inappropriate use. We can then more specifically describe the behavioral factor we initially identified (Figure 2.3).

Table 2.2   Grouping of Factors Contributing to West Nile Virus

Behavioral
Not wearing appropriate protective clothing
Not wearing long pants, long sleeves, and socks when outdoors
Being outside at dawn
Being outside at dusk
Not applying insect repellent containing DEET
Using insect repellent inappropriately
Not emptying standing water sites
Not eliminating items and places that could hold standing water
Environmental
No local mosquito control program
Lots of locations for standing water to accumulate
Nonchangable
Climate that is conducive to mosquito breeding
Geographic area that contains water for mosquito breeding

Behavioral

Not wearing appropriate protective clothing

Not wearing long pants, long sleeves, and socks when outdoors

Being outside at dawn

Being outside at dusk

Not applying insect repellent containing DEET

Using insect repellent inappropriately

Not emptying standing water sites

Not eliminating items and places that could hold standing water

Spraying repellent directly onto face

Not using enough repellent to cover exposed skin or clothing

Applying repellent to skin that is under clothing

Applying repellent to cuts, wounds, or irritated skin

Not washing treated skin with soap and water after returning indoors

Allowing children to apply own repellent

Not avoiding children's eyes and mouths, and not using it sparingly around their ears

Applying repellent to children's hands (Children tend to put their hands in their mouths.)

Not washing treated clothing before wearing again

Not using appropriate concentrations of DEET for the length of outdoor activity

Not complying with product directions for reapplication

Figure 2.3 Further defining the inappropriate use of insect repellent.

To further specify the behavior and give program planners an indication of the targets of the eventual intervention, we must clearly identify the "who" associated with the behavior. Is it a behavior that is carried out by individuals, groups, communities, caregivers, or institutions? In our West Nile virus example, parents will need to appropriately apply insect repellent to their children and be sure that their children are dressed in long pants, long sleeves, and socks when appropriate. Home owners and businesses can remove unnecessary items that can collect and hold standing water, and they can make sure that such items are otherwise emptied of water. Local government departments of public works can make sure that unnecessary items that could hold standing water are removed from public places and other water holders are emptied regularly.

The list of behavioral factors must be as specific as possible with regard to what risk behavior is being engaged in and by whom. This enables you to collect data that will help you select the best priorities for your target population and eventually make the best program objectives you can.

The behavioral factor list will identify what behaviors you will need to measure in your target population. Your needs assessment work group will have to determine which data may have recently been measured and how to get access to them; what resources you have to conduct primary data collection; what data may need to be

collected from the target population; and how and when the data will be collected. Self-report surveys, interviews, and observations can be used to collect data on behavioral factors.

Gathering primary and secondary data that are pertinent to your target population and comparison populations will help in selecting environmental priorities that are likely to have an impact if changed. If we look at our West Nile virus factors that are not behaviors we see climate, a geographic area that contains water, no local mosquito control program, lots of locations for standing water to accumulate, and the implication that mosquitoes come out most commonly at dawn and dusk. Climate, geography, and when mosquitoes come out cannot be altered. However, the lack of a local mosquito control program for an area with many mosquitoes, and the number of locations where standing water can accumulate are potentially changeable. Identifying who may have responsibility for potentially altering the environmental factors (i.e., local government agencies, individuals, and businesses) should also be identified. As with the behavioral factors, data from the target population must be collected to determine which environmental factors are present for this target group and which ones this target group perceives to be priorities. Observations, surveys, windshield tours, key informant interviews, and community forums can be used to collect this data.

Selecting Behavioral and Environmental Priorities

Once compiled and analyzed, data on behavioral and environmental factors, primary and secondary, will need to be considered with regard to importance and changeability (Green & Kreuter, 1999; Gilmore & Campbell, 1996). The importance of a factor reflects the relative strength of its contribution to the health problem, as supported by the professional literature, the factor's presence in the target population (Green & Kreuter, 1999, p. 134), and the target population's perceptions of the factor's importance (Gilmore & Campbell, 1996). Changeability refers to the likelihood that an intervention program will result in improving the factor and the target population's perceptions of the likelihood of change. Priority behavioral and environmental factors are selected based on their changeability and importance relative to the other factors on the list.

Green and Kreuter (1999) suggest the use of boxes to organize the decision-making process. Program objectives are then developed around the priority factors that are selected.

Importance, with regard to behavioral factors, represents the notions of frequency and linkage (Green & Kreuter, 1999). Those health-risk behaviors that are engaged in more frequently than others will be more important to address. So too will be those health-enhancing or health-protective behaviors that appear with low frequency in the target population or community. Importance also reflects a clear link to the health problem. The link may have been demonstrated through research or may have a strong theoretical basis. Importance may also reflect a strong desire of the target population or stakeholders to see change.

Importance, with regard to environmental factors, indicates the strength of a factor's relationship to the health problem, the incidence and prevalence of the factor, and the number of people affected by the factor. Green and Kreuter (1999) recommend considering the changeability of only those environmental factors that are considered important, because the changeability of these factors is a function of costs (economic and social) and politics. It is important to consult with your coalition members and advisory groups and, perhaps, a wider representation of the target population, given what is involved in effecting change in environmental factors.

Percentages of the population already engaging in a behavior and percentages of new initiates to the behavior reflect the frequency of the behavior in a given population. It is sometimes difficult, however, to determine what level of prevalence or incidence is problematic for the purposes of determining priorities. One simple way is to consider the health-compromising behaviors with the highest prevalence or incidence to be most important. There are many health-related behaviors that are measured and monitored regularly on local, state, and national levels. For example, the CDC developed and administers the Youth Risk Behavior Survey (YRBS) to track youth engagement in six types of behavior that are considered to be the greatest potential causes for morbidity and mortality in the US (CDC, n.d.b). These six types of behaviors are priorities in and of themselves, because of their strong links with the leading causes of death and disability. Many local school districts are part of the CDC YRBS process, and others use the survey in the community. Another way to look at the issue of frequency is to consider how the prevalence of your target group compares to some other group. Comparing the local YRBS results to those of the state as a whole or the country as a whole would indicate whether your local situation was in a better or worse position than the state or the country. Strong consideration should be given to those behaviors that are more problematic than in the state or country or both.

Relative risk and odds ratios associated with the factors on your list will assist in your priority selection, because they are measures of links between a factor and a health problem (Neutens & Rubinson, 2002, pp. 243–247). While reviewing the professional literature and other documents for factors contributing the development and continued existence of a health problem, one should note the relative risk and odds ratios associated with the factors when reported. Relative risk and odds ratios are measures of how much more at risk someone exposed to (or engaging in) a risk factor is to the health problem than someone not exposed to (or engaging in) the risk behavior. Those behavioral and environmental factors with high relative risk and odds ratios are more important to the development of the health problem than those with lower ratios. Relative risk and odds ratios may differ by subgroup, so it is important to note if there are differences by group.

The second major issue that should be considered when choosing priorities is how changeable the behavioral or environmental factor is considered to be. Changeability is a function of the resources you have available (i.e., time, money, and people), the success (or lack of success) of previous efforts to alter the factor (Green & Kreuter, 1999; Gilmore & Campbell, 1996), and the willingness of the target population to address the factor (Gilmore & Campbell, 1996). Once again, it is through the professional literature that one will determine how likely a behavior is to respond to efforts to change it. In general, the research indicates that health-risk behaviors that are being experimented with or are only newly adopted are easier to change than those deeply embedded in culture and lifestyle or those that have compulsive or addictive components (Green & Kreuter, 1999).

How do you consider both importance and changeability in a systematic way? Many suggest constructing boxes based on those recommended by Green and Kreuter (1999) (Figure 2.4).

Essentially, all the factors on your list will be placed in one of the four quadrants of the box. (Some use two boxes, one for behavioral factors and one for environmental factors.) Notice that placement is relative; factors are either more or less important or changeable. Most of the time, the priorities will be selected from the group deemed both more changeable and more important, but, as indicated in the figure, there may be situations when a factor from another quadrant is selected. Figure 2.5 presents an example of how some of the factors related to the West Nile virus example might be considered.

Other decision-making processes can be employed, such as various versions of individuals assigning weights (1 being the lowest priority and 5 being the highest priority) to each factor (or to a number of criteria for each factor) and selecting priorities based upon some predetermined cutoff (Gilmore & Campbell, 1996; Witkin, 1984). A nominal group process may also be used.

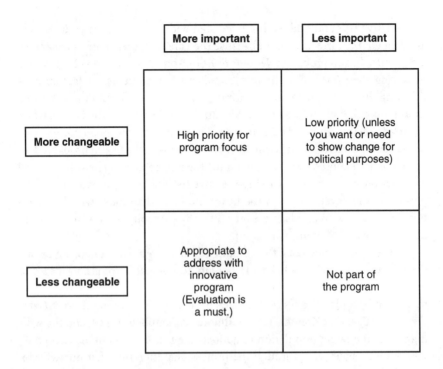

Source: Based on Green, L. W. & Kreuter, M. W. (1999). *Health promotion planning: An educational and ecological approach* (3rd ed.)(p. 138). Mountain View, CA: Mayfield.

Figure 2.4 Changeability and importance box.

No matter what decision-making process is used, the target population should be involved (Minkler & Wallerstein, 2003; Green & Kreuter, 1999). The coalition or advisory group should be included in this decision-making process. However, the factors selected should be clearly linked to the needs assessment and should be supported by gatekeepers and target population members.

In the West Nile virus example, both behavioral and environmental factors may be considered to be at least somewhat important, but it is more difficult to determine changeability. Why? Decreasing community items that hold standing water (e.g., cleaning road drains) is relatively easy to accomplish politically and has some economic cost. However, changing this environmental factor would have less impact on the health problem than implementing a mosquito control program. A mosquito control program, however important, would have higher economic costs, could potentially involve some social costs (the need to stay indoors during spraying), and could be politically difficult to support.

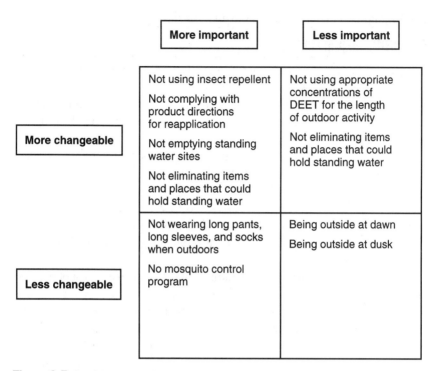

	More important	Less important
More changeable	Not using insect repellent Not complying with product directions for reapplication Not emptying standing water sites Not eliminating items and places that could hold standing water	Not using appropriate concentrations of DEET for the length of outdoor activity Not eliminating items and places that could hold standing water
Less changeable	Not wearing long pants, long sleeves, and socks when outdoors No mosquito control program	Being outside at dawn Being outside at dusk

Figure 2.5 Partial analysis of West Nile virus factors.

Perceptions of community members may be that spraying creates a high health risk itself, so the use of spraying to control mosquitoes would not be supported. Green and Kreuter (1999) remind us that many risk assessments do not reflect real risk levels. It may be necessary to explore the risk of addressing some environmental factors before final priorities are selected.

The selection of priority behavioral and environmental factors should be approached systematically. Do we always select priorities from both groups? It will depend on the specific situation. In schools and health care situations, most factors chosen will be behavioral. Community-level programs and worksite programs may have the missions and resources to address environmental factors. Members of health promotion programs should always consider addressing environmental factors. In addition, the coordinated school health program's healthy school environment component suggests that environmental factors that are contributing to health problems of students, faculty, and staff should be seriously considered for change. What remains at the end of this process are the behavioral and/or environmental factors that will receive further analysis and about which program objectives will be written.

Identifying the Contributors to Priority Behavioral and Environmental Factors

Whether you think of it as conducting an educational and ecologic assessment (Green & Kreuter, 1999) or as describing why health-risk behaviors are happening and environmental factors continue to exist, this next portion of the needs assessment will identify for you those specific elements that the program will need to address.

As with the previous portion of the needs assessment, scour the professional literature to create an exhaustive list of factors that contribute to each priority behavioral and environmental factor; group like factors together; collect data from your target population with regard to these factors (resources permitting); and prioritize and select those factors that your program will address. Objectives will then be written about the selected factors. Let us take a closer look.

Once again, the professional literature will help you create a list of the possible contributors to each of your priority behavioral and environmental factors. Literature reviews and research studies about the health problem and the priority behavioral and environmental factors will provide items for your list. Reviewing models and theories associated with health, health behavior, health education, health promotion, and the like will also provide factors for the list.

The Precede–Proceed model (Green & Kreuter, 1999) suggests grouping factors into three groups: predisposing, reinforcing, and enabling factors. The main benefit of these groupings for the program planner is that factors within each group lend themselves to change through similar types of intervention activities.

Predisposing factors include awareness, knowledge, values, beliefs, attitudes, perceived needs, and self-efficacy (Green & Kreuter, 1999). These factors exist prior to the engagement in a behavior and exist "in one's head." They can be strengthened through direct communication (Green & Kreuter, 1999, p. 156), including public media campaigns and educational activities. **Reinforcing factors** are those that reward the continued engagement in the behavior. Reinforcing factors operate after the behavior has begun. It is useful to think of reinforcing factors as mostly pertaining to people and institutions that are important to those engaging in the behavior, such as family, peers, teachers, employers, health care providers, churches, and the government. The media can also play a part in reinforcing existing behaviors. Internal reinforcing factors, such as pain or pleasure derived from the behavior, may also contribute. Interventions that facilitate role-modeling, social support, instrumental support, and the like, directed toward those people and institutions that are important to the target population, would be appropriate for promoting health-enhancing behaviors. **Enabling factors**, often environmental in nature, allow a behavior to begin or to continue or allow an institution to act. These factors include the availability, accessibility, and cost of services and goods needed to engage in a behavior or to sustain an environmental factor. Also in this category are new skills that individuals, communities, or organizations need before a new behavior can be carried out or the environmental factor changed.

It is sometimes difficult to place a factor in only one category. It may depend on the specific situation in which it appears in the community or is discussed in the literature. One may also struggle with whether an item is an environmental factor or an enabling factor. Green and Kreuter (1999) suggest that it is appropriate to place an item in as many groups as is appropriate, as long as it receives appropriate scrutiny. It is useful to see if the factor can be described more specifically or in more than one way. The resulting factors may make it easier to determine where best to place it.

Once the list of factors, categorized into three groups, has been completed, the factors that are present in the target population or community and the degree to which they are present must be determined. As in the previous step, begin by looking for existing data that describe the presence of the factors in the target group or community. Once you have gathered this information, you can determine which data will need to be collected, along with how best to collect it them. It is very important at this point to determine if varying subgroups of your target population differ with regard to the presence of the factor. Different subgroups within the target population may have different factors that need to be strengthened to achieve behavioral, environmental, or organizational changes. Surveys, questionnaires, and tests are often used to collect data from the target population about predisposing factors. These tools can also be used to establish reinforcing factors. Skills tests, surveys, and observations are often used to measure enabling factors.

Once compiled and analyzed, data on predisposing, reinforcing, and enabling factors, primary and secondary, will need to be considered with regard to importance and changeability (Green & Kreuter, 1999; Gilmore & Campbell, 1996). The importance of a factor reflects the relative strength of its contribution to the behavioral or environmental priority, along with its presence in the population (Green & Kreuter, 1999, p. 134). Changeability refers to the likelihood that an intervention program will result in improving the factor. Priority predisposing, reinforcing, and enabling factors are selected based on their changeability and importance relative to the other factors within and across groups.

The mix of predisposing, reinforcing, and enabling factors that are selected for change through program activities will depend on the specific situation with regard to resources, mission, and support from stakeholders, gatekeepers, and supervisors. There may not be sufficient monies to increase the availability of a particular service, but increasing the adoption of new skills may be a possibility. Schools may want to focus on the predisposing factors, because they are more in line with schools' missions. The coalition, advisory board, or wellness team should be involved, as always, in determining the priorities. Once selected, objectives will need to be written about these factors.

> Dee and Jose were glad they continued to assess the situation related to respiratory diseases. The coalition found out that air pollutants from the manufacturing plants a few miles away were higher in concentration than they were supposed to be, and that the worksite air conditions were not up to Occupational Safety and Health Administration (OSHA) regulations. Wow! The coalition realized that addressing this environmental factor would require community organizing. A new work group was formed to explore that avenue. Cigarette smoking was selected as the priority behavioral factor. After some long discussions, it was decided that Dee wil focus her efforts on preventing smoking initiation in all grades, but she will also work to provide smoking cessation workshops for those at the secondary level who already smoke. Jose is going to focus on smoking cessation for adults.
>
> Once the factors contributing to smoking were determined and analyzed it was decided that Jose needed to focus on decreasing those factors that were reinforcing smoking and to strengthen perceptions that emerged indicating that many people important to the adults, such as grandchildren, children, and coworkers, disapproved of the adults' smoking behavior. Jose has a rather long list of possible objectives to address with a rather large target population. Dee has a smaller target population, but is thinking about some small, intensive smoking cessation programs. They must figure out what resources they have (or can get) and identify anything that might get in the way of putting their programs in place.

Administrative and Policy Assessment

Now that you have figured out the targets of change for your program and have written preliminary goals and objectives, you can move on to the intervention. But wait! Not so fast. It is useful and important to take a look at the resources for and barriers to your program objectives and the program itself, both before and during its development. You must determine if you have the resources to (1) address all of your objectives in (2) the manner you have planned. You also must identify and remove, if possible, any barriers to implementing your program as planned (NACCHO, n.d.; Green & Kreuter, 1999).

Checkpoint 2.5

What do we mean by *resources*?

Before beginning this part of the assessment you should look at your advisory board or planning committee to see if you need to add representatives from the settings where you will likely deliver all or part of your program. Of course, a lack of resources, in and of itself, would be a barrier. So let us begin with a resource assessment.

Resource Assessment

Resources include time, money, and people. Time assessment involves determining whether sufficient time exists to meet your stated goals and objectives and whether this time has been planned for. It is also important to map out the program as it develops to see if objectives are being addressed in a time sequence that is consistent with their places in the objective hierarchy and in relation to one another. For example, an objective to increase knowledge related to a specific health problem and its causes would need to be addressed in a program before an objective related to new skill development. Both of these objectives would need to be addressed and (met to some extent) before behavior could change. Gantt charts are visual depictions of activities that are to occur across time that help us to see these relationships in graphic form. The objectives and their associated program activities are listed down the side of the chart, and a measure of time is listed across the top (in days, weeks, or months). Horizontal lines depict when specific program activities begin and end and how much time is devoted to each.

People resources largely include the level of availability and training of appropriate personnel (Green & Kreuter, 1999). Can the program be delivered with existing personnel? What percentage of their time will this program require? Are there people available who have the necessary skills to conduct various components of the program? Will you have to hire extra or outside personnel? Do you have or can you acquire the money to do so? It is important to remember to include support staff in this resource assessment.

The budget situation will also have to be assessed. The largest categories in a budget will be personnel (the largest), supplies, services, and travel (in some cases) (Green & Kreuter, 1999). Essentially, the amount of money needed is going to have to be estimated and compared to the budget the program has been given. Begin by estimating costs. Be as detailed as possible and estimate high. Use the highest prices you are quoted for supplies and services, for example.

Once costs have been estimated, available resources must be determined. Will the budget that was given to you by your school, worksite, agency, or organization be able to cover your estimated costs? If so, great! If not, how do you adjust? If you have not done so already, (1) go back and determine what appropriate materials are on hand and available for use with little or no adaptation, (2) recruit in-kind services from volunteers (who may need training), local college or university staff, college interns, and the like, and (3) recheck the cost estimates.

What if your resource needs cannot be met? Green and Kreuter (1999) recommend exploring the answers to the following questions:

- Do you know the minimum level of implementation needed to achieve your stated objectives? Check the evaluation literature.

- Are there parts of your intervention that are excessive and could be eliminated? In some instances, too much is not a good thing. Once again, be familiar with what the professional literature has to say about your strategies, methods, and targets of change.

- Is there a critical piece to the program that must happen in order for it to work a piece to which most other pieces are linked (e.g., a provision of free screenings or an extended lunch break)? If you do not have the resources to support such a piece, then the program probably is not worth putting into place.

- Can you alter the objectives (e.g., focusing on subgroups rather than the entire target population or using a longer time frame to spread costs over budget years)?

- Can you exclude or delay addressing certain objectives?

Implementation Assessment

Before committing to implementing an intervention, take a look at factors that could support or prevent successful implementation (NACCHO, n.d.; Green & Kreuter, 1999). These factors include, but are not limited to, staff support of the program, the need for staff training time if new skills are required for the intervention, the availability of appropriate space for program delivery, gatekeeper and target population comfort levels, and the acceptance of the scope and speed of the program.

Policy Assessment

Program planners must compare at the mission, policies, and regulations of your school, agency, organization, or worksite and the views of those involved in the intervention to identify whether they support and facilitate the program's implementation or whether there are any conflicts with the intended program. You may have developed the best program or the most innovative activities, but they cannot produce changes if they cannot be initiated. Does the new tobacco unit use demonstrations involving lit cigarettes and blowing smoke? It might not be able to use those activities in a smoke-free building? If conflicts are identified, the program plan must be adapted or the regulation or policy must be changed.

Checkpoint 2.6

Who would you check with, or where would you find the policies for a school district, a worksite, or health clinic?

Political forces at the national, regional, state, local, and organizational levels can affect your ability to implement your program and acquire resources (NACCHO, n.d.). For example, funding sources may direct monies toward initiatives that are politically popular and away from those that are politically unpopular. City councils and school boards may or may not approve your program or curricular initiative based on politics. Knowing ahead of time what is and is not politically supported will help program planners to decide how to proceed. Attempting to change the political viewpoint and clearing the way for your program efforts, perhaps through community organizing, may be tried. However, adapting the program may be necessary. It may be decided that the adapted program would result in a poor use of resources, making it necessary to move on.

> Jose compared his projected budget to his resources and found out that he must narrow the scope of his program. He is going to take a look at the needs assessment and see what subgroups he can target. Dee found out that she cannot run smoking cessation groups during the school day. She will have to work on promoting them in such a way that they will be attractive as an extracurricular activity.

The Big Picture

1. Gather data about quality of life, including assets and problems. Be sure to include the target group in the process, and be sure to ask the target group what it thinks throughout the entire needs assessment process. Identify and use existing data.

2. Organize and analyze the data, with the assistance of stakeholders and target group members.

3. Paint a picture of the quality of life. Identify the assets as well as the problems.

4. Gather health status data for the target population and one or more comparison populations. Be sure to ask the target population and stakeholders for their perceptions and priorities regarding health problems.

5. Look at health-related activities and services that are provided at the local level.

6. Communicate what has been found to the target population and stakeholders in an easily understandable manner. Provide a mechanism for comment.

7. Consider steps 1–7 to determine health priorities. Focus on the gaps between reality and the target group's vision of where it wants to be;

needs and available services; federal, state, and local objectives; and the current situation. Get a sense of political, economic, and technological trends, actions, and potential actions that could positively or negatively affect health status or the delivery of health services (NACCHO, n.d.).

8. Gather information from professional sources on what factors contribute to the existence and development of the priority health problems. Group factors into behavioral and environmental factors.

9. Collect data from the target population about relevant behavioral and environmental factors.

10. Use a systematic decision-making process to select priority behavioral and environmental factors. Write objectives about them.

11. Gather information from professional sources on what factors contribute to the existence of the priority behavioral and environmental factors. Group factors into predisposing, reinforcing, and enabling factors.

12. Collect data from the target population about relevant predisposing, reinforcing, and enabling factors.

13. Use a systematic decision-making process to select priority factors. Write objectives about them.

14. Conduct a resource evaluation.

When Needs Assessment Resources Are Tight

If there is a long list of potential factors and relatively few resources, one may need to collect primary data from the target population or community, measuring only those factors that seem like they would be of the highest priorities, based on your review of the professional literature. Also to be considered are the informed perceptions of your coalition or advisory board members. How should you determine about which factors to collect primary data? One way is to go to the professional literature and look at the relative risk or odds ratios for the factors' contributions to the health problem (Green & Kreuter, 1999). A relatively high relative risk or odds ratio points to a factor that should be investigated specifically with your population (Green & Kreuter, 1999). Another option is to collect data to try to validate the perceptions of your group members. You may also combine these options.

If resources exclude data collection at this point, choices will have to be based on the available information in the professional literature and any relevant existing documents. Those conducting the needs assessment must be exhaustive in the search for existing information. Depending on the size and location of the target group, it may be difficult to find existing information about the group. In that case, you will need to take at look at what is available for the "next biggest" group. For example, perhaps you are looking for existing information about some health-risk behaviors of adolescents in your school, but you cannot find any existing documents in your school that supply such information. You would next check with the school district to see if they have any recent data on adolescent health-risk behaviors. Have they recently administered the YRBS (CDC, n.d.b). Districts may administer the YRBS and only report the data by the entire district, not by individual school building. If there are no YRBS data from your district, check with your state health department. It will have the statewide YRBS data. Be sure to check that these data are from the most recent administration of the YRBS. If the most recent data are not available, it is useful to check with the CDC to see if any of the most recent data have been analyzed and use them as they become available.

Some General Reminders

The following should be kept in mind when reviewing existing documents for a needs assessment:

1. Look for and use data that are reported as rates. Rates allow us to compare groups of different sizes. Rates may be percentages or they may be reported as some number "per 10,000" (or other factor of 10). When collecting data to compare, be sure that the denominator of the rate recorded is the same. In other words, if you have a prevalence rate that is listed per 1,000 for one population, the comparison population's prevalence rate should also be listed per 1,000.

2. Obtain and record the most recent data available. You may need to find out how frequently reportable statistics are collected and reported. For example, unemployment figures are published monthly, but they are also reported by year. Incidence and prevalence rates may be reported by month, by year, or by multiple years. Some pieces of "most recent" data may be very recent—only months old—while others may be a few years old. It will depend on the collection and reporting system. Data that may be part of a previous local assessment should be updated if necessary.

3. Try to get comparison data from the same year when possible. If not, get data as close in years as possible.

4. Read the fine print on tables and graphs. It will contain important information, such as the type of information being presented, the type of rate used, and important population information.

5. Pay attention to the source of the data (Melnick, 2000). Is it a government agency, an advocacy group, or a voluntary agency? Be alert to potential biases.

6. Always note the source of the data, so it can be referenced.

Summary

Gathering, considering, and analyzing a wide variety of data about a community in order to determine its assets and needs for the purpose of setting goals and objectives is needs assessment. Needs assessment is a narrowing process that begins by painting a picture of a target population's community, with the assistance of the target population, in order to determine a program's focus. Further investigation is done to look at microlevel factors that can be changed or channeled to reach the predetermined goal. Box 2.5 provides a checklist for your needs assessment.

Box 2.5	Painting a picture of your population: A checklist to be used for each phase.

_____ Identify what information you need.

_____ Determine a timeline.

_____ Decide where, how, and from whom you will obtain the information.

    __ Read the professional literature.

    __ Identify type of data.

        __ primary   __ quantitative

        __ secondary   __ qualitative

_____ Determine who is responsible for obtaining the information.

_____ Secure needed permissions to access information from people.

    __ Consult the review board if applicable.

    __ Make sure consent letters are developed, approved, used.

_____ Identify, obtain or develop, and test data collection instruments.

_____ Collect your information.

_____ Organize your information.

_____ Analyze your information.

_____ Review analysis and set preliminary priorities.

_____ Validate priorities with target population and stakeholders.

_____ Reprioritize, if necessary.

QUESTIONS

1. Why is it important to assess the quality of life?

2. List and describe three different types of epidemiologic data that should be collected as part of a health assessment.

3. What does the term *community capacity* mean?

4. How might behavioral and environmental factors affect one another? What are some examples?

5. What are the differences between predisposing, reinforcing, and enabling factors? Why are these factors important to look at as part of a needs assessment?

6. What is meant by the term *resources?*

EXERCISES

1. Go to the Web site of your state's health department. Look at the epidemiologic data for the chronic and communicable diseases in your county. Based on the data, what conditions should be considered priorities? Justify your selection in writing.

2. Identify five potential sources of quality of life information for your community. What types of social indicators or other information for a social assessment can each provide? Make a list.

3. Access the US Census data for your county. Write a paragraph or two describing the demographics of this potential target group.

4. Locate a survey or interview instrument that is used or could be adapted to collect quality of life information about a work place. Bring it to class to discuss.

5. Write a paragraph describing the quality of life on your campus. Read it to the class and invite others' perspectives. Determine what the commonalities and differences of perceptions are.

6. Choose one of the professional journals (e.g., *American Journal of Health Education, Journal of School Health,* or *Health Education and Behavior).* Find and read an article that describes a program. From that description, list the personnel required and supplies that may be needed. Determine how much your supply budget would have to be.

7. Research the local school district policies that might impact the implementation of a coordinated school health program.

REFERENCES

Bartholomew, L. K., Parcel, G. S., Kok, G. & Gottleib, N. H. (2001). *Intervention mapping: Designing theory- and evidence-based health promotion programs.* Mountain View, CA: Mayfield.

Centers for Disease Control and Prevention [CDC], Division of Vector-Borne Infectious Diseases (n.d.a). *West Nile virus basics—Prevention: Avoid mosquito bites to avoid infection.* Retrieved April 5, 2003, from http://www.cdc.gov/ncidod/dvbid/westnile/index.htm.

Centers for Disease Control and Prevention [CDC], National Center for Chronic Disease Prevention and Health Promotion, Division of Adolescent and School Health (n.d.b). *About the YRBSS.* Retrieved April 5, 2003, from http://www.cdc.gov/nccdphp/dash/yrbs/about_YRBSS.htm.

Centers for Disease Control and Prevention [CDC]; Agency for Toxic Substances and Disease Registry, Committee on Community Engagement. (1997). *Principles of community engagement.* Atlanta, GA: Public Health Practice Program Office. Retrieved April 1, 2003, from http://www.cdc.gov/phppo/pce/index.htm.

Clark, N. (2000). Understanding individual and collective capacity to enhance quality of life. *Health Education and Behavior, 27*(6), 699–707.

Gilmore, G. D. & Campbell, M. D. (1996). *Needs assessment strategies for health education and health promotion* (2nd ed.). Madison, WI: Brown and Benchmark.

Green, L. W. & Kreuter, M. W. (1999). *Health promotion planning: An educational and ecological approach* (3rd ed.). Mountain View, CA: Mayfield.

Hodges, B. C. (1997). Those who need needs assessments and the people who have to do them: A self-help guide (Part 2). *The Catalyst, 24*(1), 2–5.

Melnick, D. (2000). *Finding and using health statistics: A self-study course.* National Information Center on Health Services Research and Health Care Technology. Retrieved July 15, 2003, from http://www.nlm.nih.gov/nichsr/usestats/index.htm.

Minkler, M. & Wallerstein, N. (2003). Introduction to community-based participatory research. In Minkler, M. & Wallerstein, N. (eds.), *Community-based participatory research for health* (pp. 3–26). San Francisco: Jossey-Bass.

Minkler, M. & Wallerstein, N. (1997). Improving health through community organization and community building: A health education perspective. In Minkler, M. (ed.), *Community organizing and community building for health* (pp. 30–52). New Brunswick, NJ: Rutgers University Press.

National Association of County and City Health Officials [NACCHO] (n.d.). *Mobilizing for action through planning and partnerships.* Retrieved July 15, 2003, from http://mapp.naccho.org/MAPPModel.asp.

Neutens, J. J. & Rubinson, L. (2002). *Research techniques for the health sciences* (3rd ed.). San Francisco: Benjamin Cummings.

Raphael, D., Steinmetz, B. & Renwick, R. (1998). *How to carry out a community quality of life project: A manual.* Toronto, Canada: University of Toronto.

Wang, C. C. (2003). Using photovoice as a participator assessment and issue selection tool. In Minkler, M. and Wallerstein, N. (eds.), *Community-based participatory research for health* (pp. 179–198). San Francisco: Jossey-Bass.

Witkin, B. R. (1984). *Assessing needs in educational and social programs.* San Francisco: Jossey-Bass.

3

Identifying and Writing Mission Statements, Goals, and Objectives

Key Terms: *philosophy, mission statement, goals, objectives*

> Dee needs to develop a program philosophy for her coordinated school health program proposal. She knows that a well-written philosophy can go a long way toward having the superintendent and the principals accept coordinated school health education. She also understands that it will help new curriculum components get accepted. But she is not quite sure how to go about it. Dee also knows that she needs to begin to write her learning and unit objectives to reflect the new state standards. She has also agreed to help Jose convert the priorities that the coalition identified into goals and objectives.

The basis or foundation of program planning is the development of a program philosophy or a strong mission statement. From the mission statement evolves the program goals and objectives, thus setting the stage for program planning, implementation, and evaluation. This critical process provides direction for the planning decisions and development of project activities that will soon follow.

The mission statement should clearly reflect the results of the needs assessment that was conducted prior to this point in the planning process. Programs may fail if decisions made by the planners are not supported by the data, or if the necessary data were not collected or reviewed by the planning committee. A good needs assessment will provide the planners with a picture of the target population, its problems, and the current or existing programs. This profile is necessary for the creation of a strong mission statement and a solid foundation for the program. Data on existing programs should be considered in order to avoid unnecessary duplication of services and to facilitate any possible joint programming efforts. Also, data obtained from previous programming efforts must be considered so that the new program can benefit from the past successes and experiences of others. The information generated from the needs assessment and its resulting analysis should be clearly reflected in the mission statement of the new program (Aspen Reference Group, 1997).

A sound mission statement must support current professional trends and reflect public health initiatives. The mission statement for the program under development and the missions of other similar health programs should have commonalities that reflect the goals that are supported or embraced by the profession. To be a part of the "global solution" it is important for health programs to share a common vision (Kreuter et al., 1998, p. 8). The Healthy People movement is an example of a professionwide goal. Healthy People 2010 (USDHHS, 2000) serves as a national agenda for the health profession and provides a translation of that common vision into goals and objectives for contemporary health education programming efforts.

What Is a Mission Statement?

The **mission statement**, or statement of purpose, is a broad statement used to present the idea of the long-term impact of the program and should be directly related to data collected during the social assessment and epidemiologic assessments as reflected in the Precede model. In order to provide that strong foundation, the mission statement must contain detailed information on the overall direction, philosophical underpinnings, and purpose of the program. The mission statement may include a brief narrative, describing the focus of the program, which often includes the program intent and philosophy description (McKenzie & Smeltzer, 2001). A good mission statement can be used for administrative purposes and provides guidance for planning and decision-making regarding the program activities and assessment of those activities (Aspen Reference Group, 1997). In addition to providing direction for the program activities, the mission statement clearly sets the stage for the organizational culture of the program for the target population, the staff, and the greater community.

Program Philosophy as the Foundation of the Mission Statement

The mission of a program may be referred to as the philosophy statement, or it may develop out of the program **philosophy**. A good philosophy statement sets the stage for the program and helps to provide the rationale and justification for its existence. In addition, the philosophy statement provides the reviewer or community member with an understanding of the beliefs or values that form the basis or framework of the program. In 1994, LaCursia, Beyer, and Ogletree identified the elements of a good philosophy statement for inclusion in a sex education curriculum. The elements identified in that research are helpful for our understanding of a philosophy that is useful for programming in many areas of health education. Elements of a good philosophy include the clear development of program beliefs or values that are founded or rooted in accurate and current information; reflective of "real life" experiences and the needs of the client; verified by experience or research; useful over time; and written in simple terminology that can be understood by the target population (LaCursia, Beyer & Ogletree, 1994). Regardless of the health education setting, a good philosophy statement will guide the planners in making sound decisions, from the establishment of the program goal to the assessment of the ability of that program to achieve that goal.

Developing a Mission Statement

The development of a useful mission statement must be one of the first major activities in the program planning process. This helps to establish the vision, scope, and direction of the project. In order to achieve program success, this step is critical. As identified by the Aspen Reference Group, "the mission statement is a public declaration of organizational beliefs, values, aspirations, and position, and it sets an attitudinal posture aimed at success" (1997, p. 205).

To assist the planner in the development of a mission statement, a list of the key elements to include in a mission statement are as follows:

1. A statement of the key elements of the philosophy, values, and program beliefs

2. A statement of the commitment the organization has to growth, stability, and survival

3. A description of the target populations and markets to be served

4. A statement of the problem to be addressed and the specific services and programs to be offered

5. A statement of the desired public image of the services or programs to be offered

As a final note on developing a mission statement, pay particular attention to the wording of the statement, as it is something that will remain as long as the program exists, if not longer. It is suggested that the planners attempt to avoid using restricting or limiting language in the development of the mission statement, or the potential of the program could be restricted or limited as well (Aspen Reference Group, 1997; Deeds, Cleary & Neiger, 1996). Box 3.1 contains examples of mission statements.

Box 3.1   Mission statement examples.

Calcutta House (Philadelphia, PA)
(http://www.calcuttahouse.org/mission.htm)

- Calcutta House exists to serve the most fragile persons with AIDS and to support the self-empowerment of each person to live, rather than give up on life.
- We provide services responsive to the individual: those who are dying and those who are able to rebuild their lives and move on to more independence.
- We work with each person to progress toward his/her potential and to achieve attainable and realistic goals.

Zero Adolescent Pregnancy (ZAP) (Cortland County, NY)
ZAP-PEERS Mission Statement
(http://www.cortland-co.org/zap/peers.htm)

- To educate, motivate, and communicate with people of all ages about self-esteem, sexuality, and responsible choices in an effort to reduce teen pregnancy rates in Cortland County.

Harvard School of Public Health (Cambridge, MA)
Global Reproductive Health Forum
Women of Color Web
(http://www.hsph.harvard.edu/grhf/WoC/mission.html)

- The Women of Color Web is dedicated to providing access to writings by and about women of color in the US. We focus specifically on issues related to feminisms, sexualities, and reproductive health and rights, although we envision adding new sections as interests arise. The site also provides links to organizations, discussion lists, and academic tools concerned specifically with women of color.
- Discussion of gender, sexuality, and reproductive health, especially on the Internet, often fail to incorporate women of color's perspectives and experiences. Although the feminist movement in the US has expanded discussion of women's rights and "choices," many have criticized the movement for focusing on the experiences of white middle-class women ignoring the needs, participation, and realities of women of color.
- Although the Internet has become an invaluable source of information, there is very little content available by and/or about women of color. Women of color voices and perspectives lack representation on this medium and little space exists for presenting and discussing ideas from women of color on gender, rights, and reproduction.
- The Global Reproductive Health Forum aims to address these concerns with the Women of Color Web by facilitating distribution and access to writings that will broaden the discussions on gender, rights, and reproduction.
- We hope this site will be useful to groups, organizations, activists, academicians, and students working or interested on these topics.

Program Goals

After finalizing the mission statement, planners then develop a program goal (or goals). To the planners, the program **goal** is that statement that provides specific long-term direction for the program. It should relate back to the quality of life and health priorities chosen during

Checkpoint 3.1

Describe in your own words how a program philosophy may set the stage for the mission or vision of a program.

the needs assessment process. Often considered a broad statement of direction, the goal is used to present the overall intent or desired outcome of a program or project. Appropriate goals and objectives help to increase the effectiveness of the planning process by helping the planners clarify the purpose and quantify realistic outcomes of the program (Deeds, Cleary & Neiger, 1996; Rainey & Lindsay, 1994).

Program goals are often written in general terms, lacking program or project specifics or details. Often, this translates into meaning that the goal is not measurable, because it lacks specific assessment criteria. This understanding of a goal differs from the understanding of program objectives, as objectives generally contain measurable specifics. Measurable specifics include such information as deadlines (e.g., by the year 2005) and disease rates or rates of increase or decrease for a health condition (McKenzie & Smeltzer, 2001; Aspen Reference Group, 1997).

Usually, the program goal is seen as a quantified statement of a desired future state or future condition. As a desired aspiration, the goal generally takes time to accomplish, which tends to translate into weeks, months, or maybe even years. Some sample program goals include the following:

- To decrease the cardiovascular morbidity and mortality rates in women older than 55 years in Our County, Massachusetts
- To decrease complications from diabetes in those age 45 years or older in Your County, Minnesota
- To decrease the prevalence of sexually transmitted infections acquired by the students of Big University
- To decrease the incidence of work-related injuries at Lee's Manufacturing

Healthy People

The efforts of health educators are often guided by the goals and objectives of the Healthy People national health promotion and disease prevention initiative. The goals of Healthy People 2010 (USDHHS, 2000) offer a model or focus for the development of goals for all health education programs. The first goal of Healthy People 2010 is to increase the quality and years of healthy life. The second goal of Healthy People 2010 is to eliminate health disparities among different segments of the population. Notice that these are broad statements that lack specifics.

Professional Philosophies and Goals of Health Education

In 1995, Welle, Russell, and Kittleson explored five philosophies in health education that are used to guide program-planning decisions. These five philosophies are called cognitive-based, decision-making, behavior change, freeing and functioning, and social change. Whichever philosophy the health education program planner subscribes to determines the development of the desired goal or outcome. A program based on the cognitive-based philosophy focuses on providing information and expanding the learner's knowledge base. The decision-making philosophy prompts a program planner to focus on the development of problem-solving skills and processes that apply to situations involving a health decision. The behavior change philosophy guides the program planner toward placing an emphasis on behavioral modification and behavior change strategies. The freeing and functioning philosophy focuses on assisting learners to make self-directed and autonomous health decisions, while emphasizing freedom, individuality, and lifelong learning. The social change philosophy utilizes education and political forces for achieving social and environmental change (Welle, Russell & Kittleson, 1995).

As the outcome or goal of the program is influenced by the philosophy of the program, it is imperative that the planners of any program clearly identify what they are trying to achieve and what they hope to accomplish. Once again, the involvement of the target population in this process is important (IOM, 2003). After the planners have clearly identified the program outcome, the mission should reflect how they hope to accomplish those goals in a way that is clearly consistent with the stated philosophy. The goal or outcome of the program must be consistent with the program philosophy and clearly linked to the mission.

Objectives

Once the program goals are in place, the planners then set about writing the program objectives. An **objective** is often defined as a specific statement of short-term application, usually written in terms that are measurable. Objectives often include activities that have a specific time limit or timeline for completion and the expected results of each activity. Each objective should be in line with a program goal and directly related to reaching that goal (Aspen Reference Group, 1997).

Types of Objectives

Program planners need to develop different types of objectives during the program planning process. Most objectives will be directed toward the individuals or institutions that will be the targets of the intervention. Other objectives should be written for the program planning and implementation staff. Different objectives, then, are directly linked to the process evaluation, the impact evaluation, or the outcome evaluation. These different types of objectives are needed to determine program success at various stages of planning and implementation. A review of the different types of objectives will follow, but, as one reads in the professional literature, it be noted that different terminology may be used to describe similar types of objectives. The important lesson to be learned is that a direct relationship between the objectives and the goals they are written to accomplish needs to exist.

Program objectives may relate to the social and epidemiologic phases of Precede and are measured as part of the outcome evaluation. Directly connected to accomplishing the project or program goal, program objectives focus on how the program will create a health change that results in changes in morbidity, mortality, and quality of life (McKenzie & Smeltzer, 2001; Deeds, Cleary & Neiger, 1996).

Action or behavioral and environmental objectives relate to the priority behavioral or environmental actions that are considered to be the cause of the health concern or issue the program is attempting to change (phase 3 in the Precede model). Measurement of the attainment of this type of objective is part of impact evaluation (McKenzie & Smeltzer, 2001; Deeds, Cleary & Neiger, 1996).

Process objectives relate to those factors examined in the process evaluation and may include two different categories of objectives, the *learning objectives* and the *administrative objectives*. Learning objectives are those objectives that reflect a desire for a change in knowledge, attitudes, or specific skills or practices. Learning objectives reflect the predisposing, reinforcing, and enabling factors identified in the educational and organizational phase of the Precede model. Administrative objectives relate to the activities of the project and the tasks that are completed along the way. Issues such as the number of sessions held, the use of appropriate materials, and attendance at activities are considered the focus of administrative objectives. These are reflected in the administrative phase of the Precede model (Green & Kreuter, 1999; Deeds, Cleary & Neiger, 1996).

Levels of Objectives

Because program objectives reflect the variety of changes that the program is attempting to accomplish, it is useful, when planning a program, to reflect the hierarchy of objectives related to the target group. In the following hierarchy of levels of objectives (Keyser et al., 1997), the lower the number assigned to the objective, the easier it is considered to create the change. In most cases, lower level objectives have to be met before higher level or more difficult ones can be attained.

1. Awareness objective: demonstrates the desire to increase the target population's awareness of a health issue or health concern.

2. Knowledge objective: demonstrates the desire to increase the target population's knowledge of a health issue or health concern.

3. Attitude objective: demonstrates the desire to produce a positive change in the target population's attitude(s) toward engaging in the health-enhancing behavior or dealing with the health concern.

4. Skill development objective: demonstrates the desire to assist the target population in developing a health skill to engage in the health-enhancing behavior.

5. Access objective: demonstrates the desire to increase the access or availability of health services for the target population.

6. Behavior objective: demonstrates the desire to change an unhealthy behavior in the target population to a health-enhancing behavior.

7. Risk reduction objective: demonstrates the desire to reduce or eliminate risk factors for the target population.

8. Health status objective: demonstrates the desire to improve the health status of the target population.

In examining the hierarchy, it is apparent that it is consistent with the Precede framework. Predisposing, reinforcing, and enabling factors (hierarchy levels 1–5) must be addressed before behaviors (level 6) will change. Risk reduction often reflects multiple behaviors (level 7), which need to change before a measurable improvement in health status can be achieved.

Developing an Objective

When developing objectives, it is suggested that the following four elements be included (Aspen Reference Group, 1997; Rainey & Lindsay, 1994):

1. Who: Identify the target population affected or expected to engage in the desired behavior or performance.

2. What: Identify the outcome to be achieved. (What is the expected result of the activity? What behavior or performance is expected? What change is anticipated or desired?)

3. How much: Identify the specific criteria for deciding when the outcome has been successfully achieved. (Include the measurement component; how much change is expected or desired?)

4. By when: Identify the time period within which the performance or behavior is expected to occur. (When will the activity be completed and the expected results or outcome take place?)

Objectives should be written in clear but simple language, should be action oriented, and should be measurable (Aspen Reference Group, 1997). Critical to the success of your program evaluation is the development of measurable objectives. Rainey and Lindsay (1994) recommended a series of questions to ask when writing measurable objectives. The following list comes from their work:

- What criteria will be used to determine how high objectives are to be set? (How much change should be anticipated?)
- Do objectives coincide with Healthy People 2010?
- What objectives have been achieved in similar projects or programs?
- Are the objectives in line with the findings from the needs assessment (such as prevalence rates, resources, and other local conditions)?

Developing objectives based on the four elements of *who* is going to do *what* by *how much* and by *when,* along with the other considerations given, will result in a list of draft-quality objectives that are ready for final consideration for effectiveness and usefulness. The following questions, which are adapted from McKenzie and Smeltzer (2001), are important to consider for each objective to determine if it is a keeper:

- Can the objective be achieved in a reasonable amount of time (keeping in mind the timeline of the program)?
- Can the objective be realistically achieved (considering the target audience and the parameters and resources of the program)?
- Is the objective consistent with the policies, procedures, and philosophy of the organization or agency?
- Does the objective violate any of the rights of those involved in the program (participants or planners)?

What might all of these objectives look like when put together with a program goal? Let us look at an example.

Program goal:

- To decrease complications from diabetes in those age 45 years or older in Your County, Minnesota

Program objectives:

- The incidence of diabetic neuropathy in those age 45 years or older in Your County, Minnesota, will decrease by 5% by the year 2009.
- Lower limb amputations resulting from diabetic complications will decease by 10% in those older than 45 years in Your County, Minnesota, by the year 2009.

Behavior and environment objectives:

- Ninety percent of the primary care physicians in the county will engage in aggressive early diabetes type II management care in accordance with professional guidelines by the end of 2004.
- Fifty percent of those diagnosed with diabetes type II will follow through with all recommended follow-up care by 2006.

Learning objectives:

- All primary care physicians in the county will know the current professional recommendations for aggressive early diabetes type II management care by the end of 2003.
- By the end of 2005, 85% of all primary care physicians in the county will believe that aggressive early diabetes type II management care is important.
- Ninety percent of those seeking recommended diabetes type II follow-up care in Your County, Minnesota, will have transportation to their health care provider.
- Eighty percent of those diagnosed with diabetes type II in Your County, Minnesota, will understand the follow-up care recommendations by the end of 2004.
- By the end of 2004, 80% of those diagnosed with diabetes type II in Your County, Minnesota, will think that it is important to receive follow-up care.
- Sixty percent of those diagnosed with diabetes type II in Your County, Minnesota, will know someone receiving follow-up care for diabetes by the end of 2006.

Once the intervention activities that will attempt to achieve the learning objectives are developed, a set of administrative objectives should be developed. Two examples of administrative objectives in this case are as follows:

Administrative objectives:

- The program staff will develop and deliver, with the assistance of the regional American Diabetes Association Office, a traveling "diabetes care update" program for primary care physicians by the end of 2003.
- All primary care physicians in Your County, Minnesota, will have attended a "diabetes care update" program by the end of 2004.

It is often useful to incorporate mission and vision statements and objectives into the program planning work plan. See Appendix 2 for an example.

Thus, by meeting the administrative objectives, the learning objectives, which will lead to the behavior and environment objectives, can be achieved. Achievement of the behavior and environment objectives will, over time, lead to achieving the program objectives and, eventually, the program goal.

Checkpoint 3.2

In general, what is the difference between a goal and an objective?

Summary

In program planning, the development of a philosophical foundation in the form of a mission statement sets the stage for all the planning, implementation, and evaluation activities that are needed for success. From the mission statement, the program goal or goals are developed, while considering the national trends or vision of the profession. In order to achieve the program goal, objectives are written that clearly provide the implementation staff with the direction necessary for the development of the activities of the program. When writing the objectives, the planners must consider the different types and levels of objectives, as different types and levels of activities are necessary in order to accomplish the desired changes and outcomes. Finally, by evaluating the effectiveness of the objectives, and ultimately the goal, the success of the program and its many activities are determined.

> Jose and Dee developed a preliminary set of goals and objectives and brought them to the next coalition meeting. During the meeting, they asked themselves the appropriate questions to assess whether the goals and objectives were appropriate, realistic, and measurable. There were a couple of behavior objectives that the group was unsure about, so they are looking in the professional literature to see what others have been able to accomplish.

QUESTIONS

1. What is a mission statement?
2. How are mission statements, program goals, program objectives, and a program philosophy related?
3. Why is it important for members of your target population to be involved in the setting of program goals and objectives?
4. What are the five philosophical positions in health education?
5. What are the different types of objectives that are needed in the program planning process?

EXERCISES

1. As a member of the planning committee for a communitywide program to decrease the rates of teen smokers, you are asked to describe the value of a well-written mission statement to the other program planners and representatives from the target population. Include in your statement a description of the relationship of the mission statement to the initial needs assessment, the development of program goals and objectives, programming efforts, and evaluation.

2. As the coordinator of worksite wellness at a large white-collar business, you are developing a new program initiative to address stress-related health problems. Write a mission statement that is appropriate for your program.

3. Go back to the list of factors associated with West Nile virus found in Chapter 2. Select appropriate factors and write a program goal and program objectives for your county.

4. For your West Nile virus program, write an objective for each type of objective offered in the chapter (program objective, behavioral and environmental objective, learning objective, and administrative objective).

5. For your worksite wellness stress management program, write an objective for each of the eight levels of objectives.

REFERENCES

Aspen Reference Group (1997). *Community health education and promotion: A guide to program design and evaluation.* Gaithersburg, MD: Aspen.

Deeds, S. G., Cleary M. J. & Neiger, B. L. (1996). *The certified health education specialist: A self-study guide for professional competency.* Allentown, PA: National Commission for Health Education Credentialing.

Green, L. W. & Kreuter, M. W. (1999). *Health promotion planning: An educational and ecological approach* (3rd ed.). Mountain View, CA: Mayfield.

Institute of Medicine [IOM] (2003). *The future of the public's health in the 21st century.* Washington, DC: National Academies Press.

Keyser, B. B., Morrow, M. J., Doyle, K., Ogletree, R. & Parsons, N. P. (1997). *Practicing the application of health education skills and competencies.* Sudbury, MA: Jones and Bartlett.

Kreuter, M. W., Lezin, N. A., Kreuter M. W. & Green L. W. (1998). *Community health promotion ideas that work: a field-book for practitioners.* Sudbury, MA: Jones and Bartlett.

LaCursia, N. L., Beyer, C. E. & Ogletree, R. J. (1994). The importance of a philosophy in sexuality education. *FLEducator, 13*(1), 4–9.

McKenzie, J. F. & Smeltzer, J. L. (2001). *Planning, implementing, and evaluating health promotion programs: A primer* (3rd ed.). Needham Heights, MA: Allyn & Bacon.

Rainey, J. & Lindsay, G. (1994). 101 questions for community health promotion program planning. *Journal of Health Education, 25*(5), 309–312.

US Department of Health and Human Services [USDHHS] (November 2000). *Healthy people 2010.* 2nd ed. *Understanding and improving health and objectives for improving health.* 2 vols. Washington, DC: US Government Printing Office.

Welle, H. M., Russell, R. D. & Kittleson, M. J. (1995). Philosophical trends in health education: Implications for the 21st century. *Journal of Health Education, 26*(2), 326–332.

4

Program Planning: The Big Picture

Key Terms: planning committee, program ownership, program desired outcome, potential program provider, potential consumer, evidence-based or science-based

> The coalition feels good about their needs assessment. What an interesting process it was, and they discovered much that they did not know. Clearly, however, respiratory-related health problems are on the rise, and cigarette smoking is by far the major contributor. Now, they have to decide what to do.

Health professionals have always planned programs to achieve desirable ends, such as to impact health status and improve the quality of life. Over the years, planning has become more systematized and, as a result, potentially more effective. The planning models developed to assist in this process include Precede–Proceed, PATCH, Model for Health Education Planning (MHEP), and Comprehensive Health Education Model (CHEM) (McKenzie & Smeltzer, 2001). Although the models differ, there does appear to be some consistency in the literature regarding recommendations for going about the program planning process. Suggested steps for program planning and general planning principles will be reviewed in this chapter. The planner may conduct the planning activities in an order that differs from the one presented here, or a number of the described activities of program planning may be conducted simultaneously. The size and past experiences of the planning committee may influence the steps for planning, along with the size and scope of the program being planned and implemented.

Box 4.1	Action steps to establish or strengthen a coordinated school health program.

At the school level	At the district level
Establish school-based leadership.	Secure district-level leadership.
Identify key players.	Establish a broad-based advisory committee.
Establish a healthy school team and select a coordinator.	Identify supports and challenges in the broader school community.
Get support from other school-site staff.	Develop supportive board policies.
Establish a common language.	Train district and community advocates to sell the program.
Set up a safety net.	
Map existing school-based and community-based resources.	
Identify student, family, and staff needs.	
Identify programmatic needs.	
Develop an implementation and coordination plan.	
Identify existing and potential sources of funding.	

Source: Fetro, J. V. (1998). Implementing coordinated school health programs in local schools. In Marx, E. & Wooley, S. F. (eds.), *Health is academic: A guide to coordinated school health programs* (p. 21). New York: Teachers College Press.

Program Planning Steps

Step 1: Review the Needs Assessment

It is suggested that the planners conduct a review of the needs assessment data and the resulting decisions that have been made up to this point. This review will help to determine if the most appropriate recommendations for the direction and outcome of the program have been made to meet the needs of the target population. It is possible for the planning committee to identify additional data that are useful to shaping the intervention, which were not undiscovered or overlooked in the initial needs assessment process. A large amount of data may have been collected as part of the needs assessment, but during a review, a skillful planning committee can organize and synthesize the information into a format that provides meaning and value, which may not have been obvious during the initial examination of the data (Aspen Reference Group, 2002).

Step 2: Convene an Advisory Panel or Planning Committee

As described in an earlier chapter, community members should be involved in the entire planning process, as they are important contributors to the development of all aspects of the program, from conducting the needs assessment to evaluating the program (Aspen Reference Group, 2002; W. K. Kellogg Foundation, 1998). For a number of reasons, it is necessary to involve or consult with appropriate community members at the very beginning of the program planning process and to include them on an advisory panel or **planning committee**. As with the needs assessment process, target population and stakeholder involvement is necessary during the planning and implementation stage. The involvement of target population members will help to develop **program ownership**, which is critical for their eventual involvement in and acceptance of the program. Target population members can provide the planners with critical insight into the target population that could make or break the efforts toward the desired outcome of the program. It is important that the program be founded on the philosophical position that it is being done *with* the community rather than *to* the community (Rainey & Lindsay, 1994).

If a coalition or advisory board was formed prior to the needs assessment, its members may form the basis for the program planning committee. When there is an existing committee structure, it will be important to review constituencies that will need to be represented for the program planning part of the process. Important contacts for inclusion on any coalition or board include **potential program providers**, as well as potential program clients or **potential consumers**. Representatives from a local college or university might also be considered, as they may offer skills and possible resources to assist with program planning and implementation. College professors might have areas of expertise that are needed by the planning committee, or a college class might assist in conducting some of the activities of the project as part of a course requirement. Consider representatives that will enhance the work of the committee and prove to be helpful to the success of the new program. When putting together a list of potential program planning advisory board members, consider individuals that can be described as follows:

- Are well respected by the target audience and can provide valuable links to the community
- Represent the various groups within your target population and have the ability to provide relevant input for program planning
- Have knowledge of the target audience, members and their lifestyles, attitudes, and resources
- Bring to your committee a number of skills and resources that will be useful to the program (Aspen Reference Group, 2002; Breckon, Harvey & Lancaster, 1994)

   To encourage a potential candidate to take a position on an advisory board
or committee, it is recommended that he or she be contacted personally through
a face-to-face discussion or telephone conversation. When a personal contact
is not possible, a letter or e-mail that reaches out to potential board members
may be necessary. Regardless of how the initial contact is made, the following
information may prove useful for informing the potential board member of the
fundamentals of the program being developed (Keyser et al., 1997):

- A statement on the purpose or intent of the contact
- The name of a key contact person, his or her title, and organization
  (including a brief overview of his or her role in this project)
- A description of the target population
- The area of emphasis of the program and the health concern or issue to be
  addressed
- Program justification
- A solicitation of support from the receiver
- Ways that the potential candidate may connect with the key contact
  (e-mail address and cell and office phone numbers)

Step 3: Assess and Establish a Budget for Program Planning

A budget must be considered for the planning phase of the project. Subsequently
in this chapter, program budgets will be addressed, but a budget for program
planning is important to facilitate the planning process. Because a budget for
planning is often overlooked, it is added here as a separate step. This step is
important, because resources are needed for conducting the initial research
and putting together the groundwork that is required prior to piloting and implementing the program. Creating an advisory or planning committee, developing the materials of the program, and preparing the necessary documents all
require staffing, time, and financial support. Program success depends on this
planning process, and cutting corners here can result in a program that fails
to meet the needs of the target population and fails to produce the **program
desired** outcome.

Step 4: Write and Review a Mission Statement

The mission statement is a narrative statement describing the focus of the program,
which often includes the program intent and philosophy (McKenzie & Smeltzer,
2001). Developing a mission statement is a critical step in creating a strong
foundation for the development of program goals and objectives and is a program activity that must be accomplished very early in the planning process. A
mission statement may have been written as part of the needs assessment process,
so it is important to review any existing mission statements before proceeding.

Step 5: Write and Review Program Goals and Program Objectives

The program goals evolve from the mission statement, and the objectives evolve from the goal or goals. Once the mission statement is in place, the task of developing the outcome or goal of the project, along with the specific objectives, needs to occur (NACCHO, n.d.). Objectives outline in measurable terms the desired changes that should occur in the target population as a result of the intervention and provide the basis of evaluation for the program (McKenzie & Smeltzer, 2001). Suggestions for developing a mission statement, program goals, and objectives are provided in an earlier chapter. If goals and objectives were developed as part of a needs assessment process, they will need to be reviewed and possibly adjusted.

Step 6: Select a Theory or Theories on Which to Base Your Program

One or more theories or specific constructs from the professional literature is needed to guide the planners in developing or selecting the intervention required to meet program goals and objectives (Glanz & Rimer, 1997). Successful health education programs are grounded in a theoretical foundation that is reflective of the current research and understandings of the profession. Chapter 6 reviews some of the most commonly used theories in health education and health promotion.

Checkpoint 4.1

What are some of the most commonly used theories and models for describing health behavior?

Step 7: Review Other Programs to Generate Program Strategy Alternatives

Those involved in the program planning process need to identify potential strategies that address the goals and objectives that have been identified (NACCHO, n.d.). To ensure success for the intervention, it is important to base the new program on other successful programs. A wide review of the professional literature and other professional documents, paying attention to programs and strategies that have been deemed successful through some type of evaluation, will help to generate a list of potential strategies and activities. Many foundations and professional associations or organizations offer lists of **evidence-based or science-based** programs that should be examined for potential use in the project. In the manual *Getting to Outcomes: Methods and Tools for Planning, Evaluation, and Accountability,* Fetterman (2000) provides a list of criteria for determining if a program is evidence-based and it includes the following:

- The degree to which the program is based upon a well-defined theory or model

- The degree to which the population serviced received sufficient interventions
- The quality and appropriateness of the data collection and data analysis procedures used
- The degree to which there is strong evidence of a cause and effect relationship

The use of science-based programs is encouraged but not always possible. There also exists in the literature programs that have demonstrated effectiveness but do not meet the science-based criteria. Practice-based programs or "best practices from the field" can be found in the professional literature in professional journals, through foundations and government organizations, and on Web sites (Fetterman, 2000). A search of best practices may provide the planners with strategies or intervention suggestions that can be adopted to meet the needs of the program or intervention being developed.

Once a literature review for successful programs has been conducted, followup telephone calls to staff associated with those programs may assist in providing additional details and insight that is not apparent in the available literature. A conversation with the appropriate staff member or director could provide the planners with feedback on a number of issues, such as the location and need for resources, overcoming implementation barriers, and evaluation strategies.

Step 8: Assess and Establish the Budget for Program Implementation

Review the financial arrangements for the program by looking at the money provided by the main funding source and any funding from another party or organization. Assess the allocated budget and its parameters to determine if it is sufficient to perform the tasks and activities of the program. Identify the resources for program implementation—those that already exist and those to be developed or purchased—and determine if they will be sufficient to achieve the program goals. The budget should include allocation for staffing, program supplies and materials, facilities and space, marketing resources, and other operational expenses (Breckon, Harvey & Lancaster, 1994).

For a more detailed examination of potential budget items and considerations, the following questions for the planners from the *Community Tool Box* located at http://ctb.lsi.ukans.edu/ are provided (Rabinowitz, 2003):

- What are the activities that will do the most to advance your cause and mission that you can carry out with the resources you have?
- How many staff positions will it take to run the activities and do it well?
- How much money will go to staffing (salary, consultant fees, fringe benefits) and from what sources will staff members be compensated?

- What else will be needed to run the program and its activities (space, supplies, equipment, phone and other utilities, insurance, travel, indirect costs, etc.)?

While attempting to identify the necessary personnel to be involved in the project, planners should consider hiring from the target population (Aspen Reference Group, 2002; W. K. Kellogg Foundation, 1998). Staffing with members of the community helps to increase program acceptance and provides valuable insight into the community and its members. For many programs, having sufficient funding is a primary concern. An investigation into the possibility of donated or shared resources with other community programs, such as building space or large equipment items, might help to address some funding limitations. Finding low-cost or donated program materials, such as curriculum and other educational items, may be possible through voluntary health agencies or government offices.

Grants and financial gifts from foundations, government agencies, community groups, and businesses is another way to increase funding for a program (McKenzie & Smeltzer, 2001). Opportunities for seeking soft money, such as grants, will require an investigation into the potential funding sources that exist and an examination of the types of projects or programs that are funded by those sources. Interviewing staff members from similar programs, contacting government offices for potential funding, and working with a local college or university and its research office are a few suggestions for getting started in the pursuit of soft money.

Step 9: Estimate Time

Often, a timetable of the specific tasks and activities of the program is developed to assist those involved in the process by informing them of when the activities are to take place and who is responsible for each activity. Planners often develop timelines that reflect the implementation and evaluation process. Including the entire planning process on the timetable can be most helpful (McKenzie & Smeltzer, 2001). Planners need to develop a timeline that flows logically, is realistic, and will assist in achieving the goal by the program deadline. In order to prepare a timeline many planners use a Gantt timeline and chart out the project activities on a day-to-day, week-to-week, or month-to-month basis. A wealth of information on this charting method exists in the professional literature and on the Web.

Step 10: Select Strategies and Activities

At this point, planners need to consider which intervention strategies and activities can best help to achieve the program goals. Again, a review of the literature for effective intervention details is an important step to consider. Several potential strategies should be identified for each objective. The selection of the strategies and activities of the intervention is a process that takes some time and investigation to successfully accommodate the target population and meet the program objectives.

Those involved in strategy selection must attempt to identify potential barriers to the implementation of each strategy identified (NACCHO, n.d.). Reviewing the needs assessment information may identify some barriers, as will a look at the professional literature. Talking with others who may have used the strategy in similar situations can also reveal potential barriers to using the strategy. The existence of implementation barriers does not rule out the use of a strategy, but the barriers must become part of the discussion of whether to incorporate a particular strategy into the program.

The program planning group should investigate, outline, and discuss the details of all strategies being considered for inclusion in the program before making final selections, based upon a mutually agreed upon set of criteria. During this process, the group should consider program strategies that accomplish the following:

- Fit with the resources and needs of the community
- Consider the beliefs, values, and practices of the community
- Reflect field testing (have shown success in the field)
- Dispel health misconceptions (Aspen Reference Group, 2002)
- May be related to other strategies under consideration
- Support the theoretical framework of the program (NACCHO, n.d.)

In the literature on successful or similar programs, there may appear references to curricula or canned interventions that can be purchased for use with the program being developed. There are a number of national curricula or health programs that have been shown to be effective and are worth consideration for adoption. According to Lohrmann and Wooley, effective health education curricula should include the following eight characteristics:

- Are research-based and theory-driven
- Include basic, accurate information that is developmentally appropriate
- Use interactive, experiential activities that actively engage students
- Provide students an opportunity to model and practice relevant social skills
- Address social or media influences on behavior
- Strengthen individual values and group norms that support health-enhancing behaviors
- Are of sufficient duration to allow students to gain the needed knowledge and skills

■ Include teacher training that enhances effectiveness (1998, p. 44)

The MAPP process suggests that, at this point in the program planning process, a report be drafted by the planning committee (NACCHO, n.d.). The report should synthesize and outline the program planning decisions. The report then becomes a written reference point for the program planning committee during the program adoption and implementation processes. It can also be shared with advisory councils, boards of directors, and the community at large.

Step 11: Plan Evaluation

By this point in the process, the development of an evaluation plan should have been initiated. Evaluation should be designed as a continuous process so that even the planning process itself is evaluated (Aspen Reference Group, 2002). It is important to select evaluation methods and questions that will facilitate process, impact, and outcome evaluation. What data need to be collected and when are they collected are critical considerations for a comprehensive evaluation. Evaluation instruments and record-keeping methods must be developed so that the necessary data are available for the evaluators (Aspen Reference Group, 2002). The planner or planners may not have the expertise and resources to conduct all phases of the evaluation, and an outside or external evaluator may need to be consulted (Rainey & Lindsay, 1994). If an external evaluator is needed for the project, it is suggested that the evaluator be brought in during the planning phase to develop the evaluation plan as early as possible in the process.

Step 12: Determine and Establish Cooperative Agreements and Linkages with Other Appropriate Community Agencies

A successful program has at its wheel a planner who knows the importance of politics and the necessity of working with the key decision-makers and other community agencies at the local level. A review of the current programming that is being offered to the target population must be conducted. Do similar programs exist for this group? Will the program meet needs not currently being met or addressed? Determine how the new program will differ, strengthen, or enhance what already exists and if avenues for collaboration are present (Fetterman, 2000; Rainey & Lindsay, 1994). Collaborative relationships for intervention development and delivery may take many forms, including an advisory committee, a consortium, a network, or a task force. The goal of this relationship must be explored, as the outcome could be that of sharing information, coordinating services for the target population, or working to advocate for a policy or environmental change.

The following questions may help in determining if there are political barriers to the program, and may help develop the potential for cooperative relationships:

- What agencies and organizations are already involved with this health concern and might perceive your program as a threat?
- What can be done to gain the support and endorsement of those agencies?
- Should a coalition of interested groups be formed to address the health concern? (Rainey & Lindsay, 1994)

Step 13: Write Component-Specific Behavior and Learning Objectives

Once the activities and strategies of the project have been identified, and possibly purchased or developed, it may be time to reevaluate the objectives. This reevaluation is useful to determine if the existing objectives are still adequate for meeting the program goal or goals. An intervention often contains a number of different components or actions that target different behaviors or environmental factors. Each component must include objectives that are specific to each targeted action or behavior. For example, if a program focuses on physical activity, diet, and exercise, then a set of objectives must be developed for each of the three sets of behaviors. One set of objectives must be targeted toward physical activity, one toward diet, and one toward exercise. At this step in the planning process, additional learning objectives may need to be written to reflect the full scope of the intervention and all that it is developed to impact.

Step 14: Pilot-Test the Intervention

Prior to a full program implementation, it is suggested that a pilot test of the intervention be conducted. A pilot test, with a small group that represents the target population, is helpful to identify potential flaws or problems with the intervention. The information that results from this step could result in corrections that could save valuable resources and time later on. Common problems that may be uncovered during a pilot test generally deal with potential flaws in the actual design or delivery of the intervention. A process evaluation of the pilot test that examines the intervention program, strategies, materials, and implementation could result in information that necessitates adjustments to the implementation (McKenzie, Pinger & Kotecki, 2002). Some questions to ask during the process evaluation of the pilot test to determine if you need to fine-tune the implementation are as follows:

- Were program materials pretested?
- Is the message appropriate for the target audience in terms of language, values, and educational levels?
- Is the message appropriate to meet the stated objectives?
- Is the program appropriate to meet the stated objectives? (Rainey & Lindsay, 1994)

- Was the intervention implemented as planned?
- Was the person conducting the intervention well received?

Step 15: Implement the Program

This step involves carrying out the activities that make up the intervention, while attempting to meet objectives and, ultimately, the program goal. Implementation can be conducted after the pilot test results are analyzed and any resulting adjustments are made to the intervention (McKenzie, Pinger & Kotecki, 2002). Once the program is revised, it is suggested that the program be phased in rather than completely implemented. McKenzie and Smeltzer (2001) offer four approaches to phasing in a program:

1. By different program offerings
2. By placing an initial limit on the number of participants
3. By choice or location within the target population community
4. By participant ability or skill level (start with beginner-level programming)

Fetro (1998) identifies several factors or program characteristics that contribute to the successful implementation of a coordinated school health program. These characteristics, if present, assist the planner of a community or health promotion program in conducting a successful implementation as well. These characteristics include a clear underlying purpose with potential outcomes; a perceived value in addressing identified needs; adaptability; replicability; consistency with the institution's mission and vision; ease of implementation; credibility with staff and the community; a capacity for broadening the knowledge base of the target population; and the potential for the program to enhance, supplement, or support existing programs (Fetro, 1998).

> Jose and Dee decided to split their programming planning efforts by creating two new committees. One will focus on community programming interventions, and the other will work with the coordinated school health program to focus on school-age youth. The coalition will continue to exist but will meet less frequently. Some coalition members have become members of the new planning committees. The planning committees have broken into smaller work groups to establish budgets, write mission statements, define goals and objectives, and research intervention ideas.

Social Marketing, Program Planning, and Implementation

Social marketing entails using marketing principles to influence the behavior of groups for the benefit of society (Goldman, 2003). Social marketing principles can assist us in developing and implementing programs that are focused, relevant to our target populations, and, thus, more apt to be successful. As you will notice as you read this chapter, we have already discussed some concepts that are included in social marketing. However, by reviewing social marketing principles, you will learn how to make connections between program development and implementation.

Several of the most important concepts of social marketing will be discussed here. You are encouraged to consult the references at the end of the chapter on your own for more detailed discussions of these concepts. These concepts are exchange, evolving behavior, marketing mix, positioning strategy, and market segmentation (Goldman, 2003; Smith, 2000; Andreasen, 1995).

Exchange

The concept of two or more entities exchanging something is considered to be the central idea of social marketing (Smith, 2000). It answers the question, I'll consider doing this for you, but what is in it for me? For example, what does the parent get out of properly using a child car seat? What does the 60-year-old get from quitting smoking, or the fully employed parent from physical activity? The implications for the program planner and facilitator or teacher are that the behavior you are asking individuals to engage in and the benefits of engaging in it must be clearly communicated to the target group and perceived by them as beneficial. A study by Hawkins and colleagues (2002) on the meanings of sexual activity for rural youth found that the term *sexual activity* did not have one consistent definition among these youth. The first steps in setting up an exchange with this group would be to determine exactly what behaviors you are trying to get the group to adopt and clearly communicate what those behaviors are in terms and language that are clear to the target group. You would then have to figure out what they would get in exchange for engaging in the recommended behaviors or, in other words, what your program will be promoting about the recommended behaviors.

Evolving Behavior

Behavior and the reasons for (or against) engaging in a behavior evolve. Thus, an intervention must evolve and adjust. For the program planner, this means conducting a process evaluation and acting on the results. It also means that needs assessments must be periodically updated. O'Donnell and colleagues (2002) found that the percentage of both male and female urban minority youth who reported ever having engaged in sexual intercourse increased from the fall to the spring of seventh grade. This may have implications for your program.

Marketing Mix

Perhaps better known as the four Ps—product, price, place, and promotion—the proper marketing mix can be crucial to the success of a program. All four elements must be analyzed and considered during program development to ascertain the best mix for the target population. All elements are employed but not necessarily to the same degree (Goldman, 2003).

Product

Product, in this case, refers to the behavior that you are trying to have the target population adopt. Goldman (2003, p. 95) suggests a series of questions to be asked about the product (behavior) you are offering to the target population. They are summarized as follows:

- What is the core product?
- What benefits of the product, valued by the program participant or student, should be offered (e.g., feeling better about oneself, experiencing fewer symptoms, gaining increased social acceptance, or generating cost savings)?
- What is the tangible product (program or intervention)? How is it packaged? What are its features? What is its style? What is its quality level?
- How can value be added to the tangible product to make it more attractive?
- What else do participants or students receive after participation?

The program planner must complete a thorough needs assessment and must thoroughly involve the target population during both the needs assessment and program planning stages in order to address the product questions.

Price

Goldman defines the concept of price as "financial, temporal, emotional, and energy cost" (2003, p. 94). Smith (2000) reminds us to consider the social cost of engaging in the behavior being promoted. The needs assessment should include strategies to identify the target group's perceived barriers to engaging in the behavior; although, sometimes these are difficult to identify up front (Goldman, 2003). The program planners can focus intervention strategies on removing or lessening the costs (real or perceived) to the target population.

Place

Checkpoint 4.2

What might be some of the costs to a traditional college-age student for abstaining from experimentation with marijuana?

The concept of place includes the places or channels used to deliver the program, which are designed to encourage the target population to adopt the product (behavior). The program planner must assess preferable and appropriate physical locations (ensuring comfort and safety), communication delivery channels, program delivery channels, and facilitator and teacher characteristics while developing the program. Where are people willing to go or definitely unwilling to go? Where do the individuals go on a regular basis, and can delivering occur there? Are there nontraditional channels that could be considered? (Goldman, 2003).

Promotion

What are you going to say about the behavior and through what channels will you say it? These questions represent the concept of promotion. It is imperative for program planners to be culturally literate with regard to the target population, to include target population members on planning committees, and to assess and pilot channels of delivery. Channels used to attract participants may include advertising, public relations activities, direct marketing, counseling, games, personal communications, and consumer promotions.

Positioning Strategy

The program planner needs to understand, from the target population's perspective, what the competition is. What is competing with the adoption of the recommended behavior? What is done instead? The competition may include other behaviors (or not engaging in particular behaviors). There may also be attitudes, beliefs, and enabling factors associated with not engaging in the recommended behavior. This suggests that the program planner must not only examine the perceived benefits and barriers of the recommended behavior, but also those of the competing actions. This way the recommended behavior can be positioned in comparison to the competing behaviors.

Market Segmentation

As described by Forthofer and Bryant (2000, p. 36) market segmentation involves "dividing a population into distinct segments based on characteristics that influence their responsiveness to marketing interventions." In health education and health promotion, market segments might be based on such factors as stage from the Stages of Change Model (described in Chapter 6), attitude toward the behavior, level of self-efficacy, or frequency of engagement in the behavior. Dividing the target population into distinct segments has several benefits, including the identification of subgroups that can realistically be reached with available resources, and the ability to develop a program that is a good fit for each segment, rather than a general fit for the whole target population.

Checkpoint 4.3

What sort of market segmentation do we use in comprehensive school health education?

The social marketing recommendations that follow have been adapted from steps outlined by Andreasen (1995):

■ Be thorough in your needs assessment. Be sure to identify competing actions and opportunities.

■ Get help with developing your social marketing strategies if you feel "lost." Hire a consultant, utilize the faculty at local colleges and universities, or recruit a marketing specialist to your advisory group.

- Address your target population's perceived barriers to the four Ps. They are not always the same as the "real" barriers that may have been identified in your needs assessment.
- Continually reassess the four Ps as your program or curriculum evolves.
- Engage in process evaluation and make adjustments based on the results.
- It is okay to start small. Try social marketing principles in small steps and see what happens.

> Jose has selected a public awareness campaign as one of the pieces of his intervention addressing cigarette smoking. He knows that he must create and communicate messages that will resonate with the adults in the community. He decides to consider a social marketing approach.
>
> Jose went back to his needs assessment data and took a look at the factors contributing to cigarette smoking to see if they differed by age, income, ethnic or cultural group, and gender. He found some interesting differences. He decided that he needed to get a little more information about what might motivate some of these groups to exchange cigarette smoking for something else. He cajoled his supervisor into funding refreshments so that he could run a few focus groups. He found the motivators to be being able to play with the grandchildren for those older than 55 years; not having to stand outside in the cold in the winter for those from ages 30 to 55 years; and saving money for those younger than 30. He plans to base his messages around these motivators. He also determined that worksites are the best places to deliver smoking cessation programs. He will have to work on trying to get employers to allow flextime or slightly longer lunches so that employees can attend during work hours.

Summary

Recommendations for program planning, along with general principles for guiding program planning, were reviewed. Fifteen steps for successful planning and implementation were discussed. Those 15 steps consisted of conducting a review of the needs assessment, convening an advisory panel, budgeting for program planning, writing the mission statement, writing the goals and objectives, selecting appropriate theories, reviewing other programs, establishing a budget for implementation, establishing a timeline, selecting strategies and activities, planning the evaluation, establishing cooperative agreements, writing component-specific behavior and learning objectives, pilot-testing the intervention, and implementing the program.

QUESTIONS

1. What should be considered when selecting strategies for inclusion in a program?
2. What are the broad steps involved in planning a health education or health promotion program?
3. What is a pilot test, and why should it be conducted?
4. Think about adult cigarette smoking behavior. What can your program give adults in exchange for quitting smoking?
5. Conduct some research and make a list of the perceived benefits of smoking for adults, and a list of the attitudes, beliefs, and enabling factors that compete with quitting. How do you think you will position not smoking?
6. Conduct some research and make a list of the perceived benefits of smoking for adolescents and a list of the attitudes, beliefs, and enabling factors that compete with quitting. How would your positioning of not smoking differ for adolescents and adults?
7. What are some nontraditional channels of delivery that could be used for smoking adults in your community or in a worksite in your community?

EXERCISES

1. Write a one-page paper describing what might be different when planning a program for a community-based program as opposed to a school-based program.
2. Locate a description of a health promotion program. Review the program based on the criteria outlined in step seven. Would you adopt all or some of the components of this program? Why or why not?
3. Locate and examine a request for proposal (RFP) from an agency or foundation to determine the types of health education projects that may be funded with soft money. Review the types of information needed to complete the proposal process.

4. Identify a health promotion program in the professional literature. Generate a list of possible budget items, and attempt to identify a low-cost way to cover some of the necessary expenses.

5. You want to make sure that you have enough money in your budget to pilot-test your program before full implementation. Write a memo to your supervisor explaining why it is important to pilot-test your program.

REFERENCES

Andreasen, A. A. (1995). *Marketing social change.* San Francisco: Jossey-Bass.

Aspen Reference Group (2002). *Community health education and promotion: A guide to program design and evaluation* (2nd ed.). Gaithersburg, MD: Aspen.

Breckon, D. J., Harvey, J. R. & Lancaster, R. B. (1994). *Community health education settings, roles, and skills for the 21st century* (3rd ed.). Gaithersburg, MD: Aspen.

Fetterman, D. (2000). *Getting to outcomes: Methods and tools for planning, evaluation, and accountability* (Volume 1). Retrieved April 10, 2003, from http://www.stanford.edu/~davidf/empowermentevaluation.html.

Fetro, J. V. (1998). Implementing coordinated school health programs in local schools. In Marx, E. & Wooley, S. F. (eds.), *Health is academic: A guide to coordinated school health programs* (p. 21). New York: Teachers College Press.

Forthofer, M. S. & Bryant, C. A. (2000). Using audience-segmentation techniques to tailor health behavior change strategies. *American Journal of Health Behavior, 24*(1), 36–43.

Glanz, K. & Rimer, B. K. (1997). *Theory at a glance: A guide for health promotion practice.* Washington, DC: US Department of Health and Human Services; US Public Health Service; National Institutes of Health.

Goldman, K. D. (2003). Social marketing concepts. In Bensley, R. J. & Brookins-Fisher, J. (eds.), *Community health education methods* (pp. 83–105). Sudbury, MA: Jones and Bartlett.

Hawkins, M. J., Davis, M., Eady, C., Rausch, S., Donnelly, J. & Young, M. (2002). Meanings of abstinence and sexual activity for rural youth. *American Journal of Health Behavior, 33*(3), 140–145.

Keyser, B. B., Morrow, M. J., Doyle, K., Ogletree, R. & Parsons, N. P. (1997). *Practicing the application of health education skills and competencies.* Sudbury, MA: Jones and Bartlett.

Lohrmann, D. K. & Wooley, S. F. (1998). Comprehensive school health education. In Marx, E. & Wooley, S. F. (eds.), *Health is academic: A guide to coordinated school health programs* (pp. 41–66). New York: Teachers College Press.

McKenzie, J. F., Pinger, R. R. & Kotecki, J. E. (2002). *An introduction to community health* (4th ed.). Sudbury, MA: Jones and Bartlett.

McKenzie, J. F. & Smeltzer, J. L. (2001). *Planning, implementing, and evaluating health promotion programs: A primer* (3rd ed.). Needham Heights, MA: Allyn & Bacon.

National Association of County and City Health Officials [NACCHO] (n.d.). *Mobilizing for action through planning and partnerships.* Retrieved July 15, 2003, from http://mapp.naccho.org/MAPPModel.asp.

O'Donnell, L., et al. (2002). Early sexual initiation and subsequent sex-related risks among urban minority youth: The reach for health study. *Family Planning Perspectives, 33*(6), 268–275.

Rabinowitz, P. (2003). *Planning and writing an annual budget.* In *Community tool box* (Part L, Chapter 43). Retrieved April 11, 2003, from http://ctb.lsi.ukans.edu/.

Rainey, J. & Lindsay, G. (1994). 101 questions for community health promotion-program planning. *Journal of Health Education, 25*(5), 309–312.

Smith, W. A. (2000). Social marketing: An evolving definition. *American Journal of Health Behavior, 24*(1), 11–17.

W. K. Kellogg Foundation (1998). *Evaluation handbook.* Battle Creek, MI: Kellogg Foundation

5

Identifying Strategies and Activities

Key Terms: intervention, strategies, activities, tailoring, cultural appropriateness, multiple intelligences, personal determinates, self-efficacy, programs that work, method

> Dee knows that she needs to look around for a smoking cessation program that has been successful with teens. However, she would like to create new grade-specific units for the smoking prevention portion of her intervention. Jose is going to be designing a public awareness campaign to go along with his smoking cessation program. He needs to decide what it will entail.

After the initial planning steps, planners must decide on the avenues for meeting the program goals and objectives. Driven by the goals and objectives, the program **intervention** is the means by which the program planners attempt to achieve the stated outcomes. The activities of the program or the experiences that the planners outline for the target population make up the intervention. The intervention may be a single activity or a series of activities designed to assist the target population in reaching the goals and objectives of the program (McKenzie & Smeltzer, 2001).

Interventions generally consist of a combination of different activities because of the complexities of what one is trying to achieve with the program. In order to change the environment or the targeted behavior, a number of activities will be required, as creating change is complex and, at times, difficult (McKenzie & Smeltzer, 2001; Green & Kreuter, 1999). If creating change in target populations were easy, then we would all be tobacco-free. Most individuals beyond grade school have been involved in one or more educational activities focusing on the negative effects of tobacco on one's health. Yet, smoking and the use of tobacco products continue to be targeted adolescent risk behaviors in the Healthy People 2010 national agenda (USDHHS, 2002).

As previously discussed, the selected activities and strategies must clearly reflect the theoretical foundation of the program. If a program is founded on a theory or model that attempts to explain or predict behavior, then the activities of the intervention should reflect the concepts or constructs from that theory or model. Thus, for example, if the program is based upon the social cognitive theory, then strategies and activities should be selected that will increase self-efficacy and improve behavioral capability (see Chapter 6).

The **activities** of the intervention are the means by which the planners apply a theory to produce the desired outcome. As indicated in an earlier chapter, a number of different influences are implicated in producing behavioral and environmental changes. A variety of different strategies and activities are necessary to effectively create the proper influence to impact the **personal determinates** and, thus, achieve the desired change. McKenzie and Smeltzer (2001) identify 11 different categories of intervention activities that planners can use in their programs to achieve the desired effect. Those categories and a brief explanation of each are offered here (adapted from McKenzie and Smeltzer, 2001):

1. Communication activities: activities that convey a message, using such media as handouts, brochures, and radio, television, or newspaper campaigns.

2. Educational activities: activities associated with the formal education process, such as in lectures, courses, seminars, and workshops.

3. Behavior modification activities: activities that use behavior change techniques to achieve a desired behavior.

4. Environmental change activities: activities that alter or control the legal, social, economic, or physical environment.

5. Regulatory activities: activities such as laws, ordinances, policies, and regulations that require individuals or groups to engage in a desired behavior.

6. Community advocacy activities: activities involving community members in the process to influence social change.

7. Organizational culture activities: activities focused on changing the environment inside an organization.

8. Incentive and disincentive activities: activities that use incentives and disincentives to influence health outcomes.

9. Health status evaluation activities: activities, such as health screenings and health-risk appraisals, that increase awareness of one's health status.
10. Social activities: activities that create social support systems for behavior change.
11. Technology-delivered activities: activities that use current technology to deliver health education and health promotion programs.

Interventions, Methods, and Strategies

As described earlier, the intervention generally consists of a number of activities selected to reflect the theoretical foundation of the program and to achieve the desired outcomes. The distinction between methods and the strategies used within the scope of the selected methods, is important to understand. The **method** is the big picture or the framework of the intervention (Gilbert & Sawyer, 2000). Consider the method as the theory-based technique used to influence the behavior or the environmental condition of the individual, the group, or the community (Bartholomew et al., 2001). The **strategies** are ways of organizing and putting into place or operationalizing the intervention method. The difference is that strategies are how health educators accomplish the methods, keeping in mind that one may incorporate a number of different strategies into the intervention for each method used. For example, if the method in the intervention is setting goals, one strategy might involve having the target group view a videotape of individuals describing how their exercise plans helped them to achieve their personal fitness goals. A second strategy might consist of having members of the target group develop a 6-month personal exercise plan.

General Intervention Considerations

Tailoring the Intervention

Getting a clear understanding of the target population, including prior knowledge, beliefs, values, personal needs, and learning styles, is important for shaping the program to meet the needs of the group and to help group members view the program as relevant. This valuable information should have been collected during the initial planning phases and should be available to the planning committee. **Tailoring** the intervention and its methods to the characteristics of the group and the individuals in the group will help to make the intervention more acceptable and also increase its potential. In other words, planners need to choose an intervention that is efficient and effective for their target population (Bartholomew et al., 2001; McKenzie & Smeltzer, 2001).

Cultural Appropriateness

In health education and health promotion, the challenge is to develop interventions that achieve **cultural appropriateness** for many different populations and communities. Meeting the needs of the target group and that group's different cultural experiences is important (Brookins-Fisher & Thomas, 2003; Gilbert & Sawyer, 2000). The following suggestions for tailoring program activities for different cultural characteristics is offered (Aspen Reference Group, 2002):

- Use a multilevel approach by incorporating different strategies that affect different levels of the problem (e.g., social, economic, and political levels).
- When translating materials into different languages, consider more than just a word for word translation. Consider a complete revision of the materials to reflect the appropriate terms and understandings of that culture.
- Organize your health promotion activities around leisure or recreational activities, community celebrations, and family-centered events.
- Incorporate different types of strategies into your intervention that use a variety of creative approaches, such as music, art, and dance.
- Try to personalize the delivery of your program, such as by carefully choosing where the intervention is offered (at a local gathering spot) or using trained facilitators from the community.
- Identify positive role models for different members (or subgroups) of the community and have them deliver the message or teach the new behavior.
- Develop messages that use clear and simple language to reach people of all educational levels.

Multiple Intelligences

Gilbert and Sawyer (2000) suggest that planners use a variety of different methods and strategies, because not all learners respond positively to the same approach. Within any group, there will be individuals with different learning styles and abilities, regardless of how similar they may appear. Dr. Howard Gardner suggests, that eight different intelligences account for human potential in both children and adults. The theory of **multiple intelligences** has strong implications for adult learning and should be considered in the selection of the intervention methods. In order to provide intervention experiences that facilitate effective learning, Armstrong (2002) suggests that the following strategies be utilized in any given intervention as a way to offer instruction that would assist all individuals in the learning process:

- Use of words, both written and spoken for linguistic intelligence
- Use of numbers or logic for logical-mathematical intelligence
- Use of pictures or visuals for spatial intelligence
- Use of music for musical intelligence

- Use of self-reflection, such as journaling, for intrapersonal intelligence
- A physical experience for bodily-kinesthetic intelligence
- A social experience for interpersonal intelligence
- An experience in the natural world for naturalist intelligence

Methods for Creating Change

In health education and health promotion, planners commonly examine methods geared toward changing personal determinates or the causes of behavior or environmental conditions. Often this examination includes intervention methods to increase knowledge, change attitudes, change social influence, and build skills and self-efficacy.

Methods to Increase Knowledge

Knowledge alone does not change behavior. However, knowledge is often considered the necessary foundation in the examination of risk perceptions, beliefs, perceived norms, and skills (Bartholomew et al., 2001). Bartholomew and colleagues (2001) offer a variety of methods for facilitating an increase in knowledge. These methods include chunking, where labels are assigned to the new information as a way to aid memory; advanced organizers, where one puts concrete examples in front of what is being learned; associated imagery or images, that involves assigning familiar images to a less familiar process; cues; tailoring of new information to concepts held by the learner; facilitated discussion; and active learning.

Methods to Change Attitudes

As a predisposing factor and personal determinate, attitude plays a role in influencing behaviors. Attitudes are related to one's beliefs, outcome expectations, perceived benefits and barriers, self-evaluation, and motivation to act (Bartholomew et al., 2001). Bartholomew and colleagues offer methods for impacting attitudes. A selection of them follows: belief selection, involving an investigation of the current beliefs of the target population; self-reevaluation or cognitive and affective assessments of self-image; environmental reevaluation, involving an assessment of how the presence or absence of a behavior affects a person's environment; arguments, involving the presentation of arguments in a persuasive message; modeling; persuasive communication; and direct experience.

Methods to Change Social Influence

Based on Ajzen's theory of planned behavior, Bartholomew and colleagues suggest that health educators have three ways to influence social expectations and social norms. First, making peer expectations known to the target population can influence normative beliefs. Second, motivation can be influenced by building resistance to the social pressure to engage in a risk behavior or by increasing motivation to comply with positive social pressure. Finally, if shifting the norm or the motivation fails to occur, attempting to shift the attention away from the behavior may prove successful (Bartholomew et al., 2001). Bartholomew and colleagues also suggest looking at mobilizing social support and modeling to create positive social influence for behavior change.

Some Common Methods for Building Skills and Self-Efficacy

Self-efficacy is seen as a crucial determinate in health behavior change. Often, methods to improve self-efficacy focus on skill development to provide individuals with the confidence (perceived skills) and the ability (actual skills) to perform a desired behavior (Bartholomew et al., 2001). The following methods are suggested for developing skills and self-efficacy: direct experience with reinforcement, modeling, guided practice, enactment, verbal persuasion, goal setting, and planning coping responses (Bartholomew et al., 2001; Kirby, 1994).

In order to provide the target population with the confidence and the ability or self-efficacy to use a skill to achieve a desired behavior, Parcel and Baranowski (1981, p. 17) suggest using the following steps in a intervention:

1. Break the behavior down into a series of tasks.
2. Teach each task as a separate skill.
3. Take small steps in successive increments.
4. Include feedback, reinforcement of appropriate procedures, and correction in each practice session with the learner.

Sources of Strategies and Activities

Finding health education and health promotion intervention strategies and activities is not a difficult task. Finding the right strategies that are appropriate for the target population and that reflect the theoretical foundation of the intervention takes time. Documentation on programs and curricula that have proven to be successful exists in the professional literature under such titles as **programs that work**, science-best programs, or best-practices programs.

As a first step, it is suggested that a review of the literature be conducted with a focus on the professional journals and documentation from government agencies that conduct research in the desired programming area. Agencies such as the CDC, the National Health Information Center, and the Institute of Medicine are just a few examples of government agencies that produce information on programming. Attending professional meetings and conferences is another way to find out what is happening in the health education or health

Box 5.1   Sample Web sites offering information on programs that work.

Resource Center for Adolescent Pregnancy Prevention
http://www.etr.org/recapp/programs/

Educational Programs that Work
http://www.ed.gov/pubs/EPTW/

International Youth Foundation
http://www.iyfnet.org/section.cfm/5

Prevention Programs that Work
http://www.usdoj.gov/kidspage/getinvolved/1_3.thm

American Council for Fitness & Nutrition
http://www.acfn.org/balance/programs.html

Teacher Talk: Programs that Work
http://www.//education.indiana.edu/cas/tt/v3i3/programs.html

promotion field regarding effective programming, new initiatives, and innovative strategies. Professional associations and health organizations, such as the American Cancer Society and the American Red Cross, also maintain publications or other material on successful programs. Looking at Web sites on programs that work or best-practices programs will assist in this process as well (Box 5.1).

Once a program (or programs) that offers intervention ideas has been identified, it is suggested that a personal contact of individuals associated with the project be conducted. Contacting planners, project directors, or grantees via the telephone or e-mail may help to provide the planners of the new program with additional information or insight into the intervention activities.

Benefits of Using Existing Materials or Curricula

Program interventions and curricula that have been used successfully are available for planners to use in their entirety or to extract strategies. One benefit of using established interventions is that, in many cases, evaluation research has been conducted and the material has proved to be successful. Planners might benefit from using materials developed by an individual who has expertise or specialized training in the development of educational materials. Often, national heath education programs or national curricula reflect current efforts and are resources for connecting with new initiatives in the field. Many proven national curricula are linked to such goals as the Healthy People 2010 national agenda and the National Health Education Standards, the national learning standards in health education. When purchasing a national program or curriculum, recipients often receive more than just a series of intervention methods or strategies. In general, purchased programs often include implementation and assessment strategies, training opportunities, periodic updates, and the possibility of online lessons or support.

Fetterman (2000) developed a checklist to assist in the process of searching out science-based programs or those programs that are believed to be effective (practice-based programs).

When considering programs, Fetterman recommends that the planners make sure that they have done the following (2000):

- Examined what science-based and best-practices resources are available in your content area
- Determined how the results of the science-based or best-practices program fit with your goals and objectives
- Determined if the results of the science-based or best-practices program are applicable to your target population (same age, similar characteristics, etc.)
- Included the evidence-based principles of effectiveness, if you are adapting a science-based program or developing a best-practices program

Tailoring Lesson Instruction

In health education or health promotion, when using canned or prepared materials, the lesson or curriculum under consideration may need to be adjusted to meet unique program needs or the needs of the target group. The following questions are suggested for creating, selecting, or improving teaching materials, such as an activity, a lesson, or a curriculum (Hedgepeth & Helmich, 1996):

- Do the materials support Healthy People 2010 and/or the national learning standards?
- Do the materials reflect current health education theories and recommendations (with a focus on behavior change or standards-based learning)?
- Is the content accurate, current, and appropriate for the target audience?
- Are the written materials appropriate for the level of the intended learner (with age appropriate instructions, reading level, and content)?
- Would the learner actively participate, finding the lessons challenging yet doable?
- Would the lessons and materials meet the needs of a diverse population?
- Would the lessons be considered fun and educational?
- Are the materials associated with the activity or lesson professionally developed?

- Does the sequencing make sense or does it need to be adjusted (from introducing the lesson concept to practicing skills)?
- Is the activity or lesson learner-centered and does it require active involvement on the part of the learner?
- Are the concepts and the skills being developed necessary?
- Does the activity provide opportunities for affective, behavioral, and cognitive development?
- Are there opportunities for ongoing assessment (from the diagnostic phase to the processing phase of the lesson)?
- Is it necessary to establish different or new ground rules before starting the activity or lesson?
- Does the room need to be adjusted or do additional props need to be used to enhance the activity or lesson?

Strategies for Health Education and Health Promotion

A variety of instructional methods, strategies, and activities are available for consideration in the intervention under development. Box 5.2 contains a comprehensive list of instructional activities for consideration in a health education or health promotion intervention.

Summary

This chapter focused on the selection of health education and health promotion methods and strategies. A number of recommendations and considerations for the location and selection of the intervention activities were provided. Recommendations included selecting methods that reflect the theoretical base of the program, provide opportunities to impact personal determinates of behavior and environmental conditions, and reflect successful interventions.

> Jose feels like he knows every antismoking public awareness campaign on the planet! (Although he knows he does not.) He read professional literature, contacted some people who had developed programs to ask questions, and paid particular attention to evaluated programs. He thinks he has put together messages and channels that will hit home with this community. Dee reviewed the major curriculum materials related to tobacco use, read widely in the professional literature, and paid special attention to best practices. With the help of their program planning committees and the entire coalition, they have put together their programs, completed some pilot-testing on them, and are ready to implement them! They have already begun the evaluation planning.

> **Box 5.2**   Commonly used instructional activities for health education and health promotion.
>
> Audiovisual material: music, voice, film (watching, critiquing, producing)
>
> Behavior change contracts and personal improvement plans
>
> Brainstorming
>
> Cartoons, humor
>
> Case studies: accident reports, hospital reports, newspaper accounts, etc.
>
> Computer-assisted instruction, use of CD-ROMs, Internet
>
> Communication: PSAs, handouts, pamphlets, announcements, displays, posters, bulletin boards, commercials, newsletters
>
> Debates
>
> Didactic approaches: lectures, discussions, computer presentations
>
> Dramatizations, skits, role-plays, vignettes
>
> Educational games and other games: BINGO, word searches, crossword puzzles
>
> Field trips, volunteer work, community assessments, field research, interviews
>
> Getting-acquainted activities: trigger activities, scavenger hunts
>
> Guest speakers, panel discussions
>
> Introspective activities
>
> Writing activities: focus writing, logs, journals, stem sentences, decision-making scenarios, essays, personification, stories, position papers
>
> Drawing, responding to pictures (nonreaders)
>
> Media: newspaper, magazines, radio, television
>
> Peers: helpers, leaders, educators, mentors, counselors, clubs
>
> Puppet shows, mascots, class family
>
> Self-appraisals, health-risk appraisals
>
> Specimens, models
>
> Stress management techniques
>
> Teachable moments
>
> Health fairs and exhibits
>
> Cooperative learning, active learning, small group work
>
> Service learning
>
> Skill development
>
> *Sources:* Gilbert, G. G. & Sawyer, R. G. (2000). *Health education: Creating strategies for school and community health* (2nd ed.). Sudbury, MA: Jones and Bartlett; Meeks, L., Heit, P. & Page, R. (2003). *Comprehensive school health education: Totally awesome strategies for teaching health* (3rd ed.). New York: McGraw-Hill.

QUESTIONS

1. Explain the difference between a method and a strategy. Give an example of each.
2. You want to be sure that your program is culturally appropriate. What are three specific actions you can engage in that will help achieve cultural appropriateness?
3. Why is it important to consider multiple intelligences when designing programs? What actions can program planners take when planning programs to address more than one type of intelligence?
4. List at least three sources for ideas about program strategies and methods.
5. What are the benefits of using existing materials or curricula?

EXERCISES

1. Visit one of the best-practices or programs-that-work Web sites. Share examples of programs and information found on the site.
2. Locate three different programs, interventions, or activities that address the same factors or personal determinates. Write a short paper explaining their similarities and differences.
3. Select a theory or model and come up with a list of possible intervention activities that reflect the different constructs presented.
4. List the possible methods and strategies that you might use in a program designed to increase the fitness levels in the residents of a 50-unit senior citizen housing complex.
5. Locate a Web site featuring a national curriculum, such as Growing Healthy, Health Skills for Life, or the Michigan Model for Comprehensive Health Education. Determine if the curriculum reflects national trends like Healthy People 2010 or the National Health Education Standards.

REFERENCES

Armstrong, T. (2002). *Multiple intelligences*. Retrieved October 24, 2002, from http://www.thomasarmstrong.com/multiple_intelligences.htm.

Aspen Reference Group (2002). *Community health education and promotion: A guide to program design and evaluation*. Gaithersburg, MD: Aspen.

Bartholomew, L. K., Parcel, G. S., Kok, G. & Gottleib, N. H. (2001). *Intervention mapping designing theory- and evidence-based health promotion programs.* Mountain View, CA: Mayfield.

Brookins-Fisher, J. & Thomas, S. B. (2003). Promoting multicultural diversity. In Bensley, R. J. & Brookins-Fisher, J. (eds.), *Community health education methods: A practioner's guide* (pp. 245–258). Sudbury, MA: Jones and Bartlett.

Fetterman, D. (2000). *Getting to outcomes: Methods and tools for planning, evaluation, and accountability* (Volume 1). Retrieved April 10, 2003, from http://www.stanford.edu/~davidf/empowermentevaluation.html.

Gilbert, G. G. & Sawyer, R. G. (2000). *Health education: Creating strategies for school and community health* (2nd ed.). Sudbury, MA: Jones and Bartlett.

Green, L. W. & Kreuter, M. W. (1999). *Health promotion planning: An educational and ecological approach* (3rd ed.). Mountain View, CA: Mayfield.

Hedgepeth, E. & Helmich, J. (1996). *Teaching about sexuality and HIV.* New York: New York University Press.

Kirby, D. (1994). *Sexuality and American social policy, sex education in the schools.* Menlo Park, CA: Henry J. Kaiser Family Foundation.

McKenzie, J. F. & Smeltzer, J. L. (2001). *Planning, implementing, and evaluating health promotion programs: A primer* (3rd ed.). Needham Heights, MA: Allyn & Bacon.

Parcel, G. S. & Baranowski, T. (1981). Social learning theory and health education. *Health Education, 12*(3), 14–18.

US Department of Health and Human Services [USDHHS] (2002). *Healthy People 2010* (2nd ed.) With *Understanding and improving health and objectives for improving health* (2 vols.). Washington, DC: US Government Printing Office.

6

The Importance and Use of Theories in Health Education and Health Promotion

Key Terms: model, theory, perceived susceptibility, perceived severity, perceived benefits, perceived barriers, precontemplation, contemplation, decision/determination, action, maintenance, reciprocal determinism, behavioral capability, reinforcement, expectations, observational learning

> Both Jose and Dee remember from when they were in college that all their professors kept using the term theory-based. Fortunately, they both remembered to take a look at some of these theories while they were developing the needs assessment plans. Several of the theoretical concepts they measured became priorities that they will address with the target populations. But how will they do that?

This chapter will give a brief overview of the use of theories in program planning. It is intended to give you some background information and examples, but it cannot, in one chapter, give you a full understanding of **theory** and its uses. At the end of the chapter, you will find a list of recommended reading to expand your understanding in this area.

What Are Theories?

Goldman and Schmalz describe theories as "summaries of formal or informal observations, presented in a systematic way, that help explain, predict, describe, or manage behavior" (2001, p. 277). Theories contain factors that attempt to describe the behaviors, explain the relationships among the factors, and outline the conditions under which these relationships exist. Some theories focus on explaining why a problem or behavior might exist, while other theories describe concepts and relationships that will help us to put a program into place in a way that will increase its likelihood of being successful and reaching its intended group (Glanz & Rimer, 1997).

Just as there are varying levels at which program planners can work to effect change, there are varying theories associated with these levels. Various theories can assist us further in identifying specific information that may be collected to more completely paint the picture of our population and our problem. Table 6.1 reviews these various levels and indicates where they may fit into the Precede–Proceed model. Table 6.2 presents commonly used theories in health at various levels and provides the related concepts we may assess or use to guide us in our planning.

Why Use Theories and Models?

Using theories help program planners think beyond the individual when conducting needs assessments and planning programs. As a result, they help planners understand the influences on health behaviors and environments (Goldman & Schmalz, 2001; Glanz & Rimer, 1997). The ability to consider factors within and beyond the individual enable program planners to select appropriate targets for interventions, develop strategies and materials that will make our interventions more successful, and save time and money (Goldman & Schmalz, 2001; Glanz, Lewis & Rimer, 1997).

How to Choose a Theory

It is important to be familiar with several theories, because not all theories will apply in all situations. One can find descriptions of theories to consider in many health education and health promotion books, in the professional literature, and as part of program descriptions. Some resources are listed at the end of the chapter. So, what does one consider when selecting theoretical concepts for in a needs assessment or as a theoretical base for a program?

First of all, consider what populations will be involved as targets of the intervention and what behaviors are being addressed (Goldman & Schmalz, 2001). When investigating theories, pay attention to the targets for which the theories were developed and on which the theories were tested. Also note the behaviors and environments to which the theories have been successfully applied.

Next, consider the purpose of the intervention under development (Goldman & Schmalz, 2001). Is the purpose to change people's behaviors or to change an environment or organization? The most powerful interventions

Table 6.1 Theory Level Relationship to Precede–Proceed Model

Level	Definition	Related portions of Precede–Proceed model
Intrapersonal factors	Characteristics of individuals affecting their behavior, including knowledge, attitudes, beliefs, personality traits, and skills	Educational and ecological assessment ■ Predisposing factors ■ Enabling factors
Interpersonal factors	Beliefs and actions of important others, including family, friends, peers, and coworkers who provide social identity, social support, and role definitions for individuals	Educational and ecological assessment ■ Reinforcing factors
Institutional or organizational factors	Rules, regulations, policies, and practices of religious, civic, social, political, and other organizations with which individuals are associated (These may constrain or support recommended behaviors or programs.)	Environmental factors Educational and ecological assessment ■ Enabling factors Administrative and policy assessment
Community factors	Formal or informal social norms, social networks, standards, or attributes that exist among individuals, groups, and organizations with which individuals are associated	Environmental factors Educational and ecological assessment ■ Reinforcing factors
Public policy	Local, state, and federal policies and laws that affect individuals' abilities to engage in health-enhancing or health-compromising behaviors	Educational and ecological assessment ■ Enabling factors administrative and policy assessment

Source: Goldman, K. D. & Schmalz, K. J. (2001). Theoretically speaking: Overview and summary of key health education theories. *Health Promotion Practice, 2*(1), 277–281; Glanz, K. & Rimer, B. K. (1997). *Theory at a glance: A guide for health promotion practice.* Washington, DC: US Department of Health and Human Services; US Public Health Service; National Institutes of Health; Green, L. W. & Kreuter, M. W. (1999). *Health promotion planning: An educational and ecological approach* (3rd ed.). Mountain View, CA: Mayfield.

Table 6.2   Examples of Theories Used in Health Education and Health Promotion

Level	Theories	Related concepts from theories
Intrapersonal factors	Health Belief Model*	Perceived susceptibility, perceived severity, perceived benefits, perceived barriers to action, and self-efficacy
	Stages of Change (Transtheoretical) Model†	Precontemplation, contemplation, decision and determination, action, and maintance
Interpersonal factors	Social Cognitive (Learning) Theory‡	Self-efficacy, reciprocal determinism, behavioral capability, reinforcement, expectations, and observational learning
Institutional or organizational factors	Stage theories of organizational change	Problem definition, action initiation, implementation of change, and institutionalization of change
Community factors	Community organization theories§	Community competence, empowerment, participation, relevance, and critical consciousness

* Strecher, V. J. & Rosenstock, I. (1997). The Health Belief Model. In Glanz, K., Lewis, F. M. & Rimer, B. (eds.), *Health behavior and health education: Theory, research, and practice* (2nd ed.) (pp. 41–59). San Francisco: Jossey-Bass.

† Prochaska, J. O., Redding, C. A. & Evers, K. E. (1997). The Transtheoretical Model and Stages of Change. In Glanz, K., Lewis, F. M. & Rimer, B. (eds.), *Health behavior and health education: Theory, research, and practice* (2nd ed.) (pp. 60–84). San Francisco: Jossey-Bass.

‡ Bandura, A. C. (1986). *Social foundations of thought and action.* Englewood Cliffs, NJ: Prentice-Hall.

§ Minkler, M. & Wallerstein, N. (1999). Improving health through community organization and community building: A health education perpsective. In Minkler, K. (ed.), *Community organizing and community building for health* (pp. 30–52). New Brunswick, NJ: Rutgers University.

will attempt to do both (Glanz & Rimer, 1997), but resources may not allow for both to be addressed.

Is the theory "logical, consistent with everyday observations, similar to those used in previous successful program examples you have read or heard about, and supported by past research in the same or related areas" (Glanz & Rimer, 1997, p. 12)? Basically, does the theory make sense in this situation (Box 6.1)?

Intrapersonal Theories

Stages of Change

The Stages of Change or Transtheoretical Model (Prochaska, Redding & Evers, 1997; Prochaska & DiClemente, 1982) concerns readiness to attempt or change a health behavior. The **model** consists of five stages of readiness that an individual moves through in the behavior change process: precontemplation, contemplation, decision/determination (sometimes called preparation), action, and maintenance. Different strategies are suggested for moving people among the different stages.

Those in the **precontemplation** stage are unaware that there is a problem and have no thoughts about changing. Thus, strategies such as health-risk appraisals, confrontations, and media campaigns that are tailored to the risks and benefits of the particular target group could be used to move them into the next stage.

Those who recognize that there is a problem and are intending to change within 6 months are said to be in the **contemplation** stage. Strategies that provide motivation to change, such as self-reevaluation, social reevaluation, and encouragement are suggested for those in this stage.

Box 6.1   Selecting theories for use in program planning.

Ask yourself these questions about any theory you are considering.
- Was the theory developed for and used with the same targets of intervention as your program?
- Has the theory been successfully applied to the same behaviors as those addressed in your program?
- Has the theory been successfully applied to the same environmental factors as those addressed in your program?
- Is the theory logical?
- Is the theory consistent with everyday observations?
- Is the theory similar to those used in successful programs you know about?
- Is the theory supported by research published in the professional literature?

Decision/determination includes those who intend to change within 30 days, have taken some steps toward change, or have made plans to change. Providing opportunities to learn goal-setting skills, to increase self-efficacy, and to obtain help in making concrete realistic change plans are strategies used to help those in this stage to act on their plans.

Those who have recently (within the past 6 months) put their change plans into effect are in the **action** stage. Social support identification and creation, reinforcement, assisting with problem-solving, and providing feedback are strategies used to help maintain the change.

When participants continue the health-enhancing action for more than 6 months, they are considered to be in the **maintenance** stage. Continued reinforcement, assistance with identifying behavioral alternatives to the former, health-compromising behavior, reminders of the benefits of the new health behavior, and help with implementing relapse plans are common strategies used for individuals and groups in this stage.

The health educator can use the Transtheoretical Model during the needs assessment to help explain reasons for engagement in health-compromising behaviors, or assess which stages the target population is currently experiencing. This information can then be used to develop an intervention with components that match strategies and materials to each stage. One can also use this information to focus the program only on those individuals in particular stages.

Health Belief Model

The Health Belief Model (HBM) (Strecher & Rosenstock, 1997) suggests to us that the likelihood of someone engaging in a recommended health action is based predominantly on individuals' perceptions. Therefore, by changing individuals' perceptions, the likelihood of those individuals acting on the health behavior recommendation increases. The four important concepts from the HBM are perceived susceptibility, perceived severity, perceived benefits, and perceived barriers (Glanz & Rimer, 1997). **Perceived susceptibility** and **perceived severity** work together to create a sense of fear related to a particular health condition. This fear is referred to as a perceived threat. **Perceived benefits** and **perceived barriers** to engaging in the recommended action are weighed, along with the perceived level of threat and self-efficacy related to the specific behavior, to produce the likelihood of action. Cues to action, such as reminder cards, may activate the behavior. Other cues, such as the appearance of symptoms, may increase the level of threat. However, this appears to be the weakest part of the model (Strecher & Rosenstock, 1997). Health education and health promotion programs are designed to increase perceptions of susceptibility and severity where appropriate, provide accurate information about benefits and barriers, reduce barriers when appropriate, increase self-efficacy, and provide cues to action.

The most appropriate uses of the HBM are for programs that are focused on a clear health problem (rather than social or economic problems), and the model lends itself well to guiding the development of messages that will encourage people to engage in recommended actions (Glanz & Rimer, 1997). Strecher and Rosenstock (1997) remind us that addressing the health beliefs of individuals and groups will be more effective than just focusing on one level.

The HBM recommended strategies include the following:

1. Conducting health-risk appraisals, presenting definitions of who is at risk, and initiating activities that prompt the target group to associate appropriate levels of risk with themselves to improve perceived susceptibility

2. Clearly and appropriately communicating the consequences of the health problem and the associated risk behavior(s) to improve perceived severity

3. Clearly and appropriately communicating what is involved in taking the recommended action (how, when, and where) and clarifying all the benefits of taking the recommended action to improve perceived benefits

4. Providing assistance with identifying and, when possible, reducing barriers to taking recommendation actions; correcting misinformation and misperceptions about barriers; and providing incentives to engage in the recommended action to improve perceived barriers

5. Reducing anxiety, demonstrating recommended actions, initiating skills training activities, giving guidance and assistance with performing recommended actions, providing role models, and providing verbal reinforcement to improve self-efficacy

> ## Checkpoint 6.1
>
> You are designing a community health program to decrease skin cancer by increasing the appropriate use of sunblock products. Develop two messages based on HBM concepts that could be included in a media campaign.

Interpersonal Theories

Social Cognitive Theory

The underlying concept of Social Cognitive Theory (SCT) is called reciprocal determinism, which asserts that a behavior arises from the continuous, bidirectional interaction of people and their environments, and that resulting behaviors, in turn, affect people and their environments (Bandura, 1986; Bandura, 1977). Glanz and Rimer explain that "the environment shapes, maintains, and constrains behavior; but people are not passive in the process, as they can create and change their environments" (1997, p. 23). For the program planner, the big message is the importance of designing programs that affect all three of those elements (people, environments, and behaviors). Though a complex theory, SCT has many useful concepts and practical application suggestions for the program planner. These are summarized in Table 6.2. You may also find these concepts under Social Learning Theory, which is an earlier version of SCT.

Looking at **expectations** and self-efficacy, SCT suggests that in order for people to engage in health-enhancing behaviors, they not only need to be confident in their ability to perform the behavior but also need to believe that the outcome of the behavior is beneficial and worthwhile (Bandura, 1986). Thus, for example, in order for a group of adult females to breastfeed their infants, they need to both be confident in their abilities to successfully breastfeed and believe that breastfeeding is beneficial to the health of their children. **Behavioral capability** is the idea that knowledge and skills influence behavior (Glanz & Rimer, 1997, p. 23; Bandura, 1986). This is why the women need to acquire knowledge about breastfeeding and training in breastfeeding skills. Perhaps, they believe that breastfeeding is uncomfortable, logistically difficult, and not worth the trouble. SCT would suggest talking with and observing others like themselves who are successfully breastfeeding. Finally, **reinforcement** can be provided for starting and maintaining breastfeeding. This may include praise from health care practitioners or breastfeeding support group members, assistance with problems from breastfeeding "buddies," or arrangments for free diapers or other infant care items.

Self-efficacy is considered to be the most important personal characteristic for influencing behavior. If I am a new mother, and I know breastfeeding is important, believe it is good for my baby, and have breastfed for the first 2 weeks of my baby's life, it is likely that I will continue to breastfeed. If I am not confident in my ability to continue to breastfeed once I go back to work, it is much less likely that I will. Those with higher self-efficacy are more likely to have the motivation to continue the behavior over time, even when confronted with barriers (Glanz & Rimer, 1997). Fortunately, there are clear strategies that appear to affect self-efficacy. According to SCT, self-efficacy can be increased by teaching people to control their negative emotional responses to performing the behavior; providing verbal persuasion and reinforcement to engage in and maintain the behavior; providing modeling of the behavior (live or through other means); making sure there are opportunities to practice the behavior in a way that will provide positive reinforcement; and ensuring the success of those engaging in the behavior (Bandura, 1977).

Behavioral capability is built by using strategies that provide knowledge about the recommended behavior and teach the skills necessary to adopt and maintain it (Bandura, 1986). Identifying positive role models and pointing out positive changes in others assist in addressing the **observational learning** concept of SCT. **Reciprocal determinism** reminds the program planner to address environmental factors and involve others who are important to the target population in the intervention. Outcome expectations, the beliefs about the results of the recommended behavior, require strategies that clearly communicate information about the likely results of engaging in the behavior. Providing positive reinforcement for steps toward and maintenance of the recommended behavior is an important strategy suggested by SCT.

Checkpoint 6.2

Your program is going to focus on increasing the use of condoms by sexually active, adolescent males. Describe two activities that may be appropriate to include in your program that would increase the condom self-efficacy of sexually active males. Be sure to describe each activity in a way that clearly links it to condom use.

Stage Theory of Organization Change

The program planner should be aware of organizational barriers to developing and implementing health promotion and health education programs. Phase five of the Precede model reminds us to assess this situation; however, being familiar with stage theories of organizational change may help avoid some barriers. These theories also offer strategies for getting a program accepted by those in charge of the approval process.

Stage theories of organizational change "explain how organizations innovate new goals, programs, technologies, and ideas" (Goodman, Steckler & Kegler, 1997, p. 288). It recognizes that organizations (e.g., school districts, worksites, and health care facilities) evolve through a series of stages, and moving from one stage to the next requires different sets of strategies and activities. These strategies and activities must be focused on those people with the power or positions to effect change. The four basic stages of organizational change are problem definition (awareness), initiation of action (adoption), implementation, and institutionalization (Glanz & Rimer, 1997).

In the problem definition stage, those in power become aware of a problem, the problem is analyzed, and ways to address the problem are investigated (Glanz & Rimer, 1997). Involving management (administrators) and others from the organization in the needs assessment process and making sure that they receive written and/or verbal summaries of problems will assist in moving the organization to the next stage.

During the initiation stage, mandates, policies, or directives that begin to address the problem are released, along with resources to begin the process (Glanz & Rimer, 1997). It is crucial at this stage to make sure that all decision-makers understand what is involved in adopting the program.

The program is then implemented, along with the process evaluation activities. It is important to ensure that those delivering the program are adequately trained and that program development staff are available to provide implementation assistance and help when problems arise (Glanz & Rimer, 1997).

Finally, when the program has become part of the organization—not something new, extra, or separate—and its goals have been internalized into the organizational culture, it is considered to be institutionalized. Institutionalization can be facilitated by developing strong supporters of the program at high levels of administration and attending to any barriers to the program's institutionalization (Glanz & Rimer, 1997).

Community Organization Theories

Community organization theories and the strategies suggested by their concepts assist the program planner when working with target groups that are underserved, lack political and economic power, and lack community organization skills (Minkler & Wallerstein, 1999; Glanz & Rimer, 1997). Empowerment and community competence are just two of the concepts included in these theories. A full discussion of these theories is beyond the scope of this chapter, and the reader is referred to the resources listed in the next section.

Other Theories

Health education and health promotion draw from a wide variety of disciplines. Thus, theories from education, psychology, sociology, anthropology, political science, economics, and marketing may all be useful in the program planning process. The program planner is encouraged to consider a variety of theories that might apply to the particular population and situation at hand. A short list of other theories that you are encouraged to investigate follows:

- Problem-Behavior Theory (Jessor & Jessor, 1977)
- Theory of Reasoned Action/Theory of Planned Behavior (Ajzen, 1998; Ajzen & Fishbein, 1980)
- Diffusion of Innovations (Rogers, 1983)
- Health Locus of Control (Wallaston & Wallaston, 1978)
- Social Marketing (Novelli, 1990)

> Dee realized that she is going to have to engage in some organizational changes to get the school district to be aware of the newer problems that the needs assessment has identified in the school-age population. Her wellness committees include school principals, but they are often too busy to attend the meetings. She will need to make sure that the principals and the superintendents all received the report prepared by the needs assessment work group. Jose is investigating other programs that have utilized SCT to get specific ideas for intervention strategies.

Summary

The consideration and use of theories and models is an important part of the program planner's need to paint a picture of the target population. Theories and models help determine factors that contribute to health behaviors in target populations, and they help program planners to think beyond the individual. The consideration of factors within and beyond the individual promotes the selection of appropriate targets for interventions and the development of strategies and materials that will make our interventions more successful, saving time and money.

QUESTIONS

1. Why is it important to use theories in program planning?
2. What strategies are associated with the HBM?
3. What is self-efficacy? Which theories is it associated with?
4. What are the benefits of using more than one theory in program planning?
5. What theories might be appropriate if one needs direction in working with an organization?

EXERCISES

1. Go back to the theoretical concepts discussed in this chapter. In which part of the Precede–Proceed model would each fit?
2. Select one or two concepts from each of the health behavior theories discussed in the chapter. Go to the professional literature and locate articles describing how others have collected data about those concepts.
3. Describe the main points of each of the health behavior theories *in your own words*. Share your descriptions with a classmate for feedback.
4. You are developing a program to increase the physical activity levels of college students on a campus. Apply this situation to each of the theories. What would each theory suggest is behind a lack of physical activity in college undergraduates?
5. Using an abstract search engine, such as PSYCH Info or the Social Sciences Index, search for an article in a professional journal that reviews the literature associated with one of the theories discussed in

this chapter. According to the article, for which target population was the theory developed and tested, and to what health behavior(s) and environments was the theory applied?

REFERENCES

Ajzen, I. (1998). *Attitudes, personality, and behavior.* Chicago: Dorsey Press.

Ajzen, I. & Fishbein, M. (1980). *Understanding the attitudes and predicting social behavior.* Englewood Cliffs, NJ: Prentice-Hall.

Bandura, A. C. (1986). *Social foundations of thought and action.* Englewood Cliffs, NJ: Prentice-Hall.

Bandura, A. C. (1977). Self-efficacy: Toward a unifying theory of behavioral change. *Psychological Review, 84*(2), 191–215.

Glanz, K. & Rimer, B. K. (1997). *Theory at a glance: A guide for health promotion practice.* Washington, DC: US Department of Health and Human Services; US Public Health Service; National Institutes of Health.

Glanz, K., Lewis, F. M. & Rimer, B. (1997) Linking theory, research, and practice. In Glanz, K., Lewis, F. M. & Rimer, B. (eds.), *Health behavior and health education: Theory, research, and practice* (2nd ed.) (pp. 19–35). San Francisco: Jossey-Bass.

Goldman, K. D. & Schmalz, K. J. (2001). Theoretically speaking: Overview and summary of key health education theories. *Health Promotion Practice, 2*(1), 277–281.

Goodman, R. M., Steckler, A. & Kegler, M. (1997). Mobilizing organizations for health enhancement. In Glanz, K., Lewis, F. M. & Rimer, B. (eds.), *Health behavior and health education: Theory, research, and practice* (2nd ed.) (pp. 287–312). San Francisco: Jossey-Bass.

Jessor, R. & Jessor, S. L. (1977). *Problem behavior and psychosocial development: A longitudinal study of youth.* New York: Academic Press.

Minkler, M. & Wallerstein, N. (1999). Improving health through community organization and community building: A health education perpsective. In Minkler, K. (ed.), *Community organizing and community building for health* (pp. 30–52). New Brunswick, NJ: Rutgers University.

Novelli, W. D. (1990). Applying social marketing to health promotion and disease prevention. In Glanz, K., Lewis, F. M. & Rimer, B. K. (eds.), *Health behavior and health education: Theory, research, and practice.* San Francisco: Jossey-Bass.

Prochaska, J. O. & DiClemente, C. O. (1982). Transtheoretical therapy: Toward a more integrative model of change. *Psychotherapy: Theory, research, and practice, 19*(3), 276–288.

Prochaska, J. O., Redding, C. A. & Evers, K. E. (1997). The Transtheoretical Model and Stages of Change. In Glanz, K., Lewis, F. M. & Rimer, B. (eds.), *Health behavior and health education: Theory, research, and practice* (2nd ed.) (pp. 60–84). San Francisco: Jossey-Bass.

Rogers, E. M. (1983). *Diffusion of innovations.* New York: Free Press.

Strecher, V. J. & Rosenstock, I. (1997). The Health Belief Model. In Glanz, K., Lewis, F. M. & Rimer, B. (eds.), *Health behavior and health education: Theory, research, and practice* (2nd ed.) (pp. 41–59). San Francisco: Jossey-Bass.

Wallaston, B. S. & Wallaston, K. A. (1978). Locus of control and health: A review of the literature. *Health Education Monographs* (Spring), 107–117.

7

Data Collection Strategies for Needs Assessments and Evaluations

Key Terms: *quantitative, qualitative, sampling, key informant, primary data, secondary data*

> Jose has organized a coalition for his substance use needs assessment and planning. The needs assessment data collection work group is ready to plan how it will obtain the data the coalition needs. Jose needs to explain to the group what its options are at its next meeting. Dee has arranged for a Saturday retreat with members of the district wellness committee who have agreed to be in charge of the needs assessment. She will be providing a workshop on data collection as part of the retreat. Jose and Dee meet together to review what the options are.

You have set up your steering committees and work groups and considered what types of information you need for your needs assessment, or, perhaps, it is time to plan the evaluation. Now comes the question, how will we get this information? You need to specify how, where, and from whom you will get data, just as you specified what types of data you need for assessments and evaluations. What are your options? What do you consider when deciding how to get your information?

Before specific options are discussed there are some terms and general actions with which you need to be familiar. **Quantitative** data are numbers. **Qualitative** data are words or pictures. Data collection methods that result in quantitative data can be analyzed through the appropriate use of descriptive and inferential statistics—counting, if you will. Qualitative data are read or observed in order to determine general themes or patterns. They are then reanalyzed to determine specific categories. Needs assessments should include both quantitative and qualitative data whenever possible.

For each part of your needs assessment and evaluation, you should seek to obtain both primary and secondary data. **Primary data** refers to data that is collected directly from people. **Secondary data** refers to data that someone else has collected and maybe even analyzed. For example, if you were putting together a data collection plan for getting information about health-related behaviors, you might administer anonymous and confidential surveys or have people complete a health risk appraisal (HRA). This is an example of collecting primary data. You might also contact your state or local health department for information from the YRBS or the Behavioral Risk Factor Surveillance Survey (BRFSS) that was administered in your area. This is an example of secondary data collection. There are lots of sources of secondary data. Once the program planning committee or evaluation committee have determined what information it is seeking, it will need to contact appropriate sources to see if they have data that are helpful.

In many cases, comparison data will be needed. Comparison data include information about a larger group and/or a similar group to which the target population belongs. Comparison data assist in determining priorities and in making decisions about what needs are the greatest and sometimes whether progress has been made. Does your group have a higher or lower incidence rate than the state as a whole? What about the United States as a whole? What about compared to similar communities or schools in the same state? Is a health-risk behavior declining in your local population but increasing in the state? For needs assessments, secondary data is usually used for making these comparisons. The ability to answer these questions will help the working groups make decisions that make the most sense for the target population.

Deciding on Data Collection Strategies

Quality needs assessments and evaluations are based on collecting, organizing, and considering as much appropriate information as possible. However, in reality it is often difficult to gather and collect all the data that are identified as being needed. Thus, decisions about what data are essential and what data collection strategies are appropriate and available to the particular needs assessment will need to be made. The resources available to you and certain characteristics of the people from whom you will collect information should be considered when making data collection decisions.

Resources

Prior to conducting any needs assessment or evaluation, a thorough determination of the available resources should be made. Knowing what resources are available ahead of time will aid in making systematic decisions when mapping out the needs assessment and evaluation plans. Systematic decisions will lead to gathering information with sufficient breadth and validity to give you a clear picture of the target population. This will increase the likelihood that the resulting intervention will have a positive impact.

Resources, in this case, means time, money, and people. These should be considered separately and in interaction with one another. The more time you have, the fewer people you may need; if you have a lot of money to work with, you may be able to hire extra people; if you have a lot of time, you may be able to seek and obtain additional funding; and so forth. Some questions to ask about resources as you begin to plan your data collection include the following:

- How much time do you have to collect the data?
- How many paid staff members and volunteers are available, and what percentage of their time can be devoted to the data collection?
- How much training will have to be provided before data collection can begin?
- What data analysis strategies have the staff and volunteers had previous experience with?
- Are there professionals in your area who are available to assist with data collection and/or analysis? Will they do it for low cost or for free?
- Do you have money to hire experts to assist with the parts of the process you and your staff might be less comfortable or familiar with?
- What technology, hard and soft, do you have access to that would assist you in the process and analysis?
- Is funding available to purchase technology or technological assistance to support data collection and analysis strategies?

As you will see, some data collection strategies are more labor-intensive than others or require certain pieces of equipment and technology. In general, primary data collection will cost more than secondary and will take longer. The more people you want to collect data from, the longer it will take and the more staff it will require. Obtaining technical assistance may cost you money and may cause you to be dependent upon others' schedules. All these factors should be considered when planning your needs assessment.

People Characteristics

Considering the individual, group, and environmental characteristics of those who you may potentially include as subjects or sources of any data will also help you make data collection decisions. One of the first questions you should ask is "how accessible is this group or person to me? Sitting down and interviewing a CEO of a large company about her potential barriers to establishing a worksite wellness program for her employees may be desirable, but it may be likely that you cannot get an appointment with her. Similarly, perhaps you are planning to measure the level of health-risk behaviors in a middle school, but district officials will not allow you to ask the students anything about their health-related behaviors. If individuals and groups are not accessible to you, you may need to switch to relying on secondary sources of information about them or people similar to them.

Developmental levels, reading ability, and cultural factors also must be considered when selecting data collection strategies. For example, self-administered surveys and questionnaires will be inappropriate for prereaders, English-only questions will often be inappropriate for nonnative speakers, and private face-to-face interviews may be culturally unacceptable if the interviewers are strangers.

Likely data collection environments should also be considered prior to the final selection of data collection plans. Will it be necessary to ensure privacy in order to do a health screening or to ask behavior questions as part of a face-to-face interview? If so, can that be arranged? Is there a space large enough to hold a community forum? Is the necessary audiovisual equipment available in all locations or can it be transported?

By doing a little preliminary work and identifying the level of resources available to you, you will be able to make informed decisions about how and from whom you will collect information.

Checkpoint 7.1

You need to get some information about the dietary behaviors of preschool children in a multiethnic community. What are some of the people characteristics you will need to consider in planning to get this information about this group?

Strategies for Secondary Data Collection

Secondary data collection is primarily done through a review of existing documents and records. The potential challenges are to identify whether current, useable data already exist, where they might be located, and how to get access to them. The advent and growth of the World Wide Web has made locating and accessing appropriate secondary data, especially state-level and national-level data, relatively easy. State departments of health, the CDC, and the National Center for Health Statistics all have Web sites that provide an abundance of health and health-related data that can be important for your needs assessment. The greater challenge is to locate current, useful information about your local area or your target population. Your coalition and advisory board members can help to identify, locate, and access existing records and documents that may be pertinent to the data collection needs (Table 7.1).

Table 7.1   **Some Common Sources of Secondary Data for Needs Assessment in Health Education and Health Promotion**

World Health Organization	US Census Bureau
Bureaus of labor statistics (federal, state, and local)	Centers for Disease Control and Prevention
Departments of health (state and local)	National Center for Health Statistics
Chambers of commerce	Health Resources and Service Administration
Divisions of social services	Local and state area health education centers
National, regional, and local offices of voluntary agencies and organizations	Law enforcement agencies (federal, state, local)
United Way offices	Voluntary organizations
School district offices	Local hospitals

When deciding whether existing information is useful, a number of factors must be considered. First of all, how old is the information? Dated information probably does not reflect the current situation and can lead you to make inappropriate decisions regarding priorities and outcomes. Second, how was the original information collected? (Goldman & Schmalz, 2000). Information that is collected anonymously and confidentially will more likely reflect the "real" situation than information that can be linked to specific individuals or groups. Third, systematic data collection procedures instituted by trained data collectors will gather useable information of quality. Data that have been gathered without a plan or by those without training will generally inaccurately reflect whatever was measured. Finally, from whom was the information collected? Is this the group about which you need information? Did a sufficient number of group members provide information to represent the entire group? Are the data reported by subgroups? If so, are the subgroups the same or similar to the ones about which you need information?

Strategies for Primary Data Collection

After identifying what information is needed and considering available resources and characteristics, data collection strategies are selected. Some strategies are more appropriate and more commonly used for certain types or sources of data (Tables 7.2 and 7.3). Often, we want to collect information in more than one way. The best way to get a feel for which strategies are appropriate is to read articles describing needs assessments, evaluations, and other research studies in the professional literature. Noting how others collected data from particular groups, about certain factors, or in different environments will provide ideas about which strategy may be appropriate in your situation.

Table 7.2   Commonly Used Data Collection Techniques for Needs Assessment

Portion of the needs assessment	Potential type of data	Primary data collection techniques	Potential secondary data sources
	Sociodemographic data	Focus groups	Departments of labor
	Socioeconomic data	Key informant interviews	Local and state departments of health
Community profile	Numbers and types of service and civic organizations	Community forum	Human resource departments
Quality of life asssessment	Child care options and facilities	Survey or questionnaire	Criminal justice organizations
Community assets Identification	Vital statistics	Newspaper analysis	School districts
	Crime statistics	Windshield tours	
	Unemployment rates	Photo novella	
	Health insurance patterns		
	Health care options and services		
	Perceptions of quality of life		
	Government structure		
	Mass transportation options		
	Climate		
	Natural resources		
	Green space		
	Recreation options		
	School test data		
Health status	Morbidity and mortality data	Focus groups	World Health Organization
	Years of potential life lost data	Key informant interviews	Local and state departments of health
	Disability data	Community forum	Health care practicioners
	Incidence rates	Survey or questionnaire	School nurse records
	Prevalence rates		Centers for Disease Control and Prevention
	Health problem distribution		

Table 7.2   Commonly Used Data Collection Techniques for Needs Assessment   (Continued)

Portion of the needs assessment	Potential type of data	Primary data collection techniques	Potential secondary data sources
Health status	Community perceptions of health problems Hospital discharge data	Collecting data on perceptions of community	Voluntary organizations Clinic records Hospital records National Center for Health Statistics (NCHS) Mental health services and facilites USDA
Risk factors	Health-related behaviors Preventive Treatment Environmental Social Physical	Survey or questionnaire Observations Focus groups Artifact analysis (garbageology) Interviews Windshield tours Plate waste studies	Local and state health departments Environmental health divisions Local school districts CDC Voluntary organizations EPA Institutional offices of environmental health and safety OSHA NIOSH USDA
Contributing factors	Knowledge Attitudes Beliefs Values Perceptions Self-efficacy	Surveys, questionnaires, or tests Observations Focus groups Skills assessments Document review	Community agency directories Local school districts Local and state health departments United Way

(Continued)

Table 7.2   Commonly Used Data Collection Techniques for Needs Assessment (Continued)

Portion of the needs assessment	Potential type of data	Primary data collection techniques	Potential secondary data sources
Contributing factors	Behaviors of important others		
	Media influences and message		
	Social support levels		
	Peer influence		
	Message for health care providers		
	Physical sensations		
	Accessibility, availability, and affordability of recommended health-related goods and services		
	Accessibility, availability, and affordability of community services necessary to take recommended health actions		
	Law, policy, and regulation enforcement		
	Personal health skills		
	Community organization skills		

Table 7.3	Commonly Used Data Collection Techniques for Evaluation	
Process evaluation	Impact evaluation	Outcome evaluation
Surveys and questionnaires	Surveys and questionnaires	Document review
		Interviews
Facilitator logs	Participant logs	Surveys and questionnaires
Participant logs	Photo novella	
Windshield tours	Focus groups	Focus groups
Photo novella	Key informant interviews	Key informant interviews
Reflection papers		
Focus groups	Interviews	Observation
Key informant interviews	Observation	Windshield tours
	Document review	Photo novella
Observation		
Document review		
Group consensus techniques		

The rest of this chapter describes a few of the more common primary data collection strategies used in needs assessments and evaluation. These are followed by a discussion of strategies used for selecting the people from whom planners and evaluators will get the information.

Observations

Observations—seeing and hearing events, situations, and behaviors—are often used to measure behaviors, but they may also be used to assess some environmental factors and contribute to an assessment of quality of life (WHO, 2000). Planners and evaluators may want to observe individuals or groups of people in order to record a number of behavioral "events" and skills, or they may want to record the behaviors of interest that individuals and groups engage in every so many minutes (Kerlinger, 1988). Communities, neighborhoods, schools, or other particular locations can be visited to note observable environmental factors, community assets, and indicators of quality of life.

The benefits of using observation include the ability to witness behaviors, skills, and conditions rather than relying on self-reports and the ability of a trained observer to document that which is of interest in the "real world," potentially improving interpretation and the ability to prioritize or assess. Its weaknesses include the possibility of the observer making incorrect observations and interpretations and the subjects of observations reacting to the presence of the observer (Kerlinger, 1988).

Observation may sound like a simple way of recording information. However, in order to make sure the information is representative and free from bias, those directing data collection need to make sure observers are seeing and hearing events in the same way and to devise ways to systematically record what is seen and heard.

Special Considerations When Using Observations

Using observations as part of a data collection plan requires advanced planning to minimize observer bias and maximize consistency across observers with regard to what is being seen (interobserver reliability), especially when attempting to observe behavior. First, the behavior that is going to be observed must be clearly identified. Let us say you tell your observers that smoking is the behavior that they will record. Does this mean smoking cigarettes, cigars, marijuana, or all three? Without clearly stating that cigarette smoking is the behavior of interest, your observers may be recording different behaviors. This does not give you a true picture of cigarette smoking in your population of interest.

Second, systematic methods to record observations as they are occurring should be used. Checksheets, logs, and formal unstructured field notes can be used to record and track the behavioral and environmental factors being measured.

Third, data collection planning should also consider how the observers can remain as unobtrusive as possible while making their observations. Visits to potential observation sites may be necessary to determine where observers should be placed.

Finally, all observers should be trained. Trainers need to ensure that all those making observations clearly understand what specific behaviors are being recorded, are familiar with the data-recording sheets and procedures, and know how to be unobtrusive. Observers should be given opportunities to practice observing before beginning data collection. Training might include having observers' watch a video and practice observing and recording what they see. Comparing observations from the video provides a means to check on observers' abilities to see the behavior that has been defined and agree with one another. Following video practice with field practice will provide added competence and increase the reliability of the observations.

Windshield Tours and Photo Novella

Windshield tours and photo novella can be effective ways to contribute to assessing both assets and issues of your target group or community, or, they can serve as part of an evaluation. Windshield tours are usually conducted by professionals (often with the assistance of trained community members) and involves driving, walking, or cycling through the target area on different days and at different times during the day, observing and recording what is observed (Eng & Blanchard, 1990). The general impressions of maintenance of buildings and grounds, the location and amount of recreational and green space, types and conditions of housing, sites where people congregate, and the amount and types of social interactions and observable health-related behavior can be recorded (Sharpe et al., 2000). Observations are usually recorded as written notes of key observations. The use of laptop computers, videotape and audiotape recorders, and maps may be employed to record observations and impressions.

Photo novella is used in needs assessment to document and reflect the needs of people to "promote dialogue, encourage action, and inform policy" (Wang & Burris, 1994, p. 172). It is used to record the perceptions of people in the target group who have little or no contact with policy makers. Members of the target population receive training in the purposes of the needs assessment and the use of the cameras. Then, they are given cameras and told to take pictures of their homes, workplaces, communities, and any other places where they spend considerable time. The photographs are developed, and the photographers provide verbal or written explanations of their photos. This information is then used as part of the needs assessment where appropriate. Photo novella can be an important tool in eliciting perceptions from marginalized groups, but it can also be useful in gathering the perceptions of adolescents. In one photo novella project, members of a youth club were given cameras and told to go out and take pictures of what was good and bad in their neighborhood. For the bad, they were instructed to find ways to illustrate what is bad without including pictures of individuals engaged in doing bad things. After the pictures had been taken and developed, the youths met in small groups. The group members were asked to comment on what they thought of each picture and why they had those thoughts. This process was used as a way to analyze and document what the group members saw as the needs and assets in their community (Goslin, n.d.).

Interviews

The interview technique can be used with individuals and with small groups, and it can be especially useful with children and subliterate populations. During an interview, a data collector asks individuals or small groups a series of questions. Interviews can be either structured or semistructured. Structured interviews consist of the interviewer asking a set of predetermined objective questions, much like what would be found on a written questionnaire (Isaac & Michael, 1981). They are usually relatively brief. Structured interviews are most useful when straightforward, factual information is being sought.

The National Association of Black and White Men Together (NABWMT), in conjunction with the University of Maryland Minority Health Education Lab, conducted structured interviews with a convenience sample of black and Hispanic gay and bisexual men found in social settings where men met or had sexual encounters with other men (Thomas & Hodges, 1991). Local members of NABWMT chapters underwent 8 hours of training to be interviewers. Interviewer training included role-play activities and direct observations of pilot interviews. Interview data were used as part of a needs assessment to plan AIDS education programs for this population.

Semistructured interviews are those in which the interviewer has a core set of questions to ask, but has the ability to ask follow-up questions to probe and clarify responses. For example, an interviewer of a human resources director of a large business might ask a question such as, "Does your company provide any programs, activities, or facilities to promote and facilitate physical activity for your employees?" If the answer is "yes," the interviewer could (1) ask for the programs to be identified, then (2) ask why the most successful program worked and why the least successful didn't work.

Individual Interviews

Although we generally think of individual interviews as being conducted face-to-face, they may also be conducted over the telephone, via video conferencing, and by electronic mail. Individual interviews are personal, can be flexible, and, when conducted face-to-face, allow for the inclusion of nonverbal responses in data gathering and analysis (Isaac & Michael, 1981). However, interviews are time-consuming, can be expensive, and can be affected by the interviewer and interviewee interaction (Neutens & Rubinson, 2002).

E-mail and telephone interviews allow the inclusion of participants that could not otherwise be interviewed because of distance or time constraints (Neutens & Rubinson, 2002; Selwyn & Robson, 1998), and they may be safer for the interviewer than conducting face-to-face interviews in dangerous locations (Neutens & Rubinson, 2002). Also, the likelihood that respondents will react to the interviewer's gender, race, age, or other characteristics in a way that can impact question responses is reduced or eliminated with both of these techniques. E-mail interviews are generally less expensive than face-to-face or telephone interviews. Respondents can reply at their convenience, and those who would otherwise be reluctant respondents may feel more comfortable answering questions electronically. The fact that e-mailed iinterview data do not have to be transcribed before analysis is an advantage in that it saves time and money and decreases potential error. However, e-mail interviews are limited to those with computer and e-mail access and cannot include the nonverbal responses that are often an important part of the data (Selwyn & Robson, 1998). In addition, ensuring anonymity may be problematic.

Telephone interviewing gives the advantage of being able to call back those who initially were not there to respond and may be better than face-to-face interviewing for collecting information about sensitive topics such as health-risk behaviors (Neutens & Rubinson, 2002). Those conducting telephone interviews must contend with hang-ups and suspicions of being a telemarketer. Computer-assisted telephone interviewing (CATI) allows the interview questions to be displayed on a computer screen and moves the interviewer through the question set depending on the response. The interviewer enters responses directly into the computer software. CATI has been found to increase the accuracy of data collection and streamline the analysis, because data are ready to be analyzed once entered. Telephone interviewing can be quite expensive, depending on the number of participants, the use of CATI, and the number of interviewers required.

Key informant interviews are commonly used in needs assessments. Key informants are those people in the community or target group or those working with the community or target group who have access to information about the group (WHO, 2000). These interviews seek to gather information about the community or target group—not the informant's personal perceptions. Conducting a number of key informant interviews can provide a range of sources that may represent the variety of the group of interest. Key informant interviews may also be useful in identifying potentially controversial areas, as well as providing guidance on how to address these areas in ways that will be acceptable. Interviewing mayors, school principals, business CEOs, officers of social and fraternal organizations, and law enforcement officers are examples of key informant interviews.

As with observations, those who will be conducting the interviews should receive training. Interviewer training should include an overview of the needs assessment or evaluation project, a review of the interview questions, and practice (Box 7.1).

Box 7.1   Basic steps for conducting individual interviews.

1. Determine the information needed or wanted to be collected via individual interviews.
2. Determine who will be interviewed, and how they will be selected and contacted.
3. Develop the interview questions.
4. Pilot-test interview questions and revise as needed for acceptability, length, and ability to get the information needed.
5. Determine the process for getting permission to interview, and obtain any permissions required.
6. Select those to be interviewed, and set up the interview times and places.
7. Train your interviewers.
8. Conduct interviews according to plan.
9. Compile responses by question.
10. Analyze responses by question.

Data analysis for individual interviews will depend on the nature of the questions. Objective, structured question formats may require no more than adding up the number of responses in certain categories. Semistructured interviews will involve the generation of transcripts and a data analysis plan that calls for the reading of the transcripts by several readers to identify reccurring themes and concepts.

Group Interviews

Group interviews are generally conducted face-to-face but can also be conducted by electronic mail and in electronic chat rooms (Selwyn & Robson, 1998). Group interviews are useful when group interaction is necessary to generate more in-depth responses or when one needs to reach a consensus. They can also be used when time and money are short.

Focus Group Interviews

A focus group interview or discussion is a qualitative approach to learning about your intended audience (Goldman & Schmalz, 2001). Focus groups are frequently used in health education (Torabi & Ding, 1998), especially as part of the program planning process (Goldman & Schmalz, 2001).

Participants in a given focus group are usually alike with regard to one or more characteristics, such as geographic location, age, gender, sociocultural orientation, risk status, or health problem characteristics. Most often, they do not know one another, but this is not always the case (Goldman & Schmalz, 2001). The composition of the groups depends on the purpose of the focus group interview. Potential participants can be randomly selected or recruited from the defined subgroups. However, respondents should remain anonymous during the group discussion, usually using first names only (Goldman & Schmalz, 2001), and data should be confidential.

Focus group interviews are conducted by a moderator, with assistance from an observer. The moderator poses questions and stimulates discussion, using a prepared outline of questions or topic areas. The observer records nonverbal responses to questions and notes any other characteristics of the discussion that would not be apparent from an audiotape or videotape. Written transcriptions are made of the discussions and put together with notes made during and immediately after the interviews, so that analysts can interpret the responses in order to ascertain the trends, recommendations, opinions, and feelings of the group with regard to the questions asked.

Analysis of focus group data involves several people reading through the written details of the focus groups to determine trends, recommendations, opinions, and feelings with regard to the questions asked. If the groups were audiotaped or videotaped, then written transcripts should be prepared to help

---

Box 7.2   Basic steps for conducting focus groups.

1. Develop questions and probes.
2. Produce script.
3. Identify and recruit moderators and observers.
4. Train moderators and observers.
5. Secure site(s) for focus group interviews.
6. Secure all needed materials.
7. Select and recruit participants.
8. Send participants a reminder letter, or give them a reminder phone call.
9. Arrive early.
10. Check the audio or video system, set up the room, and put out refreshments.
11. Conduct focus groups according to plan.
12. Thank the participants, and distribute any participation incentives.
13. Write field notes.
14. Analyze data across groups.

---

organize the information. Software, such as NUD*IST (QSR International), The Ethnograph (Scolari), or ATLAS.ti (Scolari) can also be used.

It is beneficial to run several focus groups that consist of representatives of different subgroups in your population as part of a needs assessment. For example, if you are conducting a needs assessment that is to provide data to plan or revise a school health education curriculum, several focus group interviews would be planned. As part of a curriculum revision process, Baltimore County, Maryland, conducted focus groups with middle school students and school nurses to identify perceived health education needs and perceived risk associated with a number of health-risk behaviors (Hodges, 1992). One focus group per grade level was conducted in each of three schools that were identified by the district. These groups consisted consisting of students that were randomly selected and stratified by gender. A separate focus group was also run, which consisted of school nurses who volunteered to participate in the process. The Cortland County (New York) Health Department conducted focus group interviews with teen mothers, adolescents, senior citizens, employees of local manufacturing plants, residents of the outlying rural towns, stay-at-home parents, and working single mothers as part of a needs assessment for CVD prevention intervention planning (Hodges, Videto & Gefell, 2001).

For a detailed review of the nuts and bolts of conducting focus groups see Goldman and Schmalz (2001). Basic steps for conducting focus groups are listed in Box 7.2. An example of a focus group moderator's guide can be found in Appendix 3.

Special Considerations for Interview Techniques

It is imperative that an interviewer or moderator is able to establish a good rapport with respondents, create a comfortable environment, use active listening skills, and encourage responses by those who may be reluctant to answer. Interviewers should receive training that includes role-playing.

Anonymity can be a concern for the respondents. It is more likely that individuals have been specifically chosen and, thus, are known to the interviewer, as in key informant interviews. For the purposes of transcripts, participants in a focus group must have a name, and some may be wary if the focus group is audiotaped or videotaped. Providing reassurance that none of the information will be reported with anyone's name attached to it, using first names only, and having participants make up a name for the purpose of transcript identification can be helpful.

Interviews with children may be facilitated by using "thumbs up or thumbs down" or props or pictures that the children can point to as a response to a question (Hodges, Videto & Gefell, 2001).

Written Surveys and Questionnaires

Surveys and questionnaires generate self-report data through written responses to a standard set of questions. The data generated can be quantitative or qualitative, depending on the nature of the questions. Surveys and questionnaires are quick and easy to administer and can be given to large numbers of people at once. They can be administered by paper and pencil, over the telephone, through the mail, or electronically through e-mail or Web pages. The advantages and disadvantages to using these methods are summarized in Table 7.4.

Checkpoint 7.2

Name three surveys that were administered nationally to measure health-related behaviors.

Special Considerations When Using Surveys and Questionnaires

Developing a survey or questionnaire that will measure or collect the information you really want involves more than just putting some questions down on a piece of paper. It requires a long and involved process (Box 7.3). Whenever possible, adapt and use existing surveys that others have developed and tested to see if they work (Thompson & McClintock, 1998).

Search the professional literature to identify surveys and questionnaires that were used or developed to measure the same concept or attribute on which you need information from a similar population. Once they have been identified, look to see how closely the group on which it was used matches the group on which it will be used. Consider age, literacy level, language, culture, and other characteristics that might affect the ability of the target group to truly understand the questions that are being asked. Consider also the survey's

Table 7.4   **Advantages and Disadvantages to Using Various Types of Surveys and Questionnaires**

Type of survey or questionnaire	Advantages	Disadvantages
Paper and pencil	Easy to administer Relatively inexpensive	Potential language and literacy bias Requires trained administrators
Mail	Economical High degree of anonymity is possible Respondent completes at his or her convenience Can access geographically wide populations Can increase accuracy, because respondents can check records	Lower response rates Higher likelihood of unanswered questions Cannot control order in which questions are answered
Telephone	Can be cheaper than mail Rapid response Can access geographically wide populations High degree of anonymity is possible Follow-ups (to increase response rate) less expensive and time-consuming than mail surveys	Large numbers of subjects may be expensive Incomplete data or no response may result from hang-ups No way to verify that respondent meets necessary characteristics Requires trained administrators
E-mail	Easy to administer Economical Potentially rapid response Easy to conduct follow-ups	Response rates may be low (easy to delete) Not all potential respondents have e-mail access
Web-based survey	Economical Potentially rapid response Data can be analysis ready Can access geographically wide populations High degree of anonymity is possible	May need to hire a developer Not all potential respondents have access May need to notify potential respondents by e-mail Controlling access may be difficult

Box 7.3	Instrument development process.

1. Delineate and clearly define the measurement objects.
2. Determine the target population.
3. Utilize a theoretical framework or conceptual model.
4. Develop a table of specifications.
5. Determine the purpose of the measurement.
6. Determine the types of items needed.
7. Generate a list of items from a variety of sources.
8. Establish criteria for an item's selection and refinement.
9. Develop preliminary scales with more items than needed.
10. Have the preliminary scales reviewed by a jury of experts.
11. Revise the preliminary scales.
12. Administer the scales to a representative sample.
13. Conduct an extensive item analysis.
    - Discrimination
    - Reliability
    - Validity
14. Select, refine, and prepare the final scale.
15. Administer the scale to a larger sample.
16. Perform analyses for psychometric evidence
    - Face, content, construct validity
    - Instrument reliability

properties; has it been tested for reliability and validity, and what were the results and were they acceptable? Once a survey, or a portion of one, has been selected, its use should be pilot-tested for use with the target group. The pilot test should determine whether the survey is acceptable for use with your population (from the perspective of stakeholders and the target population itself) and whether it can be completed in an appropriate and available amount of time. If at all possible, measures of reliability should be conducted with the target population.

When using surveys and questionnaires, one must plan ahead of time how anonymity and confidentiality are going to be ensured. Anonymity and confidentiality provisions must be clearly communicated to the respondents and respected by the data collectors and analyzers. Not requiring names or other identifiers on the survey instrument itself is the usual method of maintaining anonymity. If respondents need to be kept track of for the purposes of targeted follow-up to increase response rates, tracking mechanisms that are separate from the survey itself should be used. Sending preaddressed and stamped postcards to be returned when the completed survey has been mailed and keeping completion check-off lists consisting of names or identification numbers that are separate from the instrument are common ways to maintain anonymity.

Plans for obtaining high response rates should be made before conducting the survey. How will follow-ups to remind those selected to respond be conducted? Who will be responsible? How long will you wait for surveys to be completed? Sending reminder postcards for mail surveys or reminder e-mails for electronic surveys to all those selected in 2-week intervals is common. Providing an incentive for completing the survey may also help, provided that you have a separate way of tracking completion other than having respondents identify themselves on the survey itself.

An anonymous mail survey was used to gather information about characteristics of rural primary caregivers who smoke and their receptivity to family-based health promotion programs in a rural county in North Carolina (Tilson, et al., 2001). The survey, with a fifth-grade reading level, consisted of questions from existing adult health-risk behavior surveys and was adapted from a similar survey given to the children in school. It was piloted-tested with groups of parents in urban and rural areas and revised as suggested by the pilot study. All adult caregivers of children in grades four and six who were enrolled in school in the spring of 1999 were mailed the survey. The mailing included a cover letter that explained the purpose of the survey and a small incentive of five postage stamps. A second mailing was sent 2 weeks later asking the adults to fill out and return the survey if they had not done so. Mailing lists were provided by the elementary schools.

As with all forms of research, you will need to find out whose approvals are required in order to conduct your survey. Does your agency or school district have a review board that must approve your data collection plans and approve access to the population? When conducting surveys in schools, what type of parental approval is necessary? Do parents have to give active consent by returning a permission slip, or can you include all students whose parents have not returned a slip indicating that their child cannot participate (passive consent)? You must be ready to show those who give permission to conduct surveys and access the population a detailed outline of your procedures.

The directions for administration and completion of the survey are vital to its success. Wording and consistency are crucial. Standard directions for those administering the survey should be developed, written down, and pilot-tested. The directions given for completing the

Checkpoint 7.3

You have selected a questionnaire to collect information about the availability and accessibility of tobacco products to adolescents from high school students. Whose permission do you need to get in order to administer the survey? How will you obtain this permission? What will you do to ensure that the responses are anonymous and confidential?

survey must be clearly written at an appropriate level for each section of the survey. These too should be part of any pilot test.

The survey itself should be appealing to the respondents in appearance and format. Appropriate font sizes, enough white space, quality reproduction, appropriate pictures for preschool, primary-grade, and subliterate populations can increase completion rates.

Techniques for Coming to a Group Consensus

Nominal group process and the Delphi technique are useful in identifying problems and setting priorities within a group (Jackson, Pitkin & Kington, 1998; Ziglio, 1996; Duffield, 1993). Both work toward bringing the group to a consensus regarding the question or problem at hand.

In the Delphi technique, a series of questionnaires are designed and sent to a selected group involved in the decision-making process (Duffield, 1993). Questionnaires can be sent by mail or e-mail. Questions can be broad and open-ended, such as "What do you see as the biggest health problems in this community?" or specific and closed-ended, such as "Available data indicate that the following health-risk behaviors are being engaged in by adolescents in this community at higher rates than the state as a whole. Rank the list from 1, the behavior in greatest need of being changed, to 8, the behavior of lowest need to change." Responses are sent back for analysis before the next questionnaire is constructed and sent. Subsequent questionnaires summarize the previous round's responses and pose a new, more refined question related to the decision being sought. The process continues until a consensus is reached.

Nominal group process can be used to provide structure to the process of a group that is making a decision about complex issues and allows for all perspectives to be heard and considered (Jackson, Pitkin & Kington, 1998). Participants are selected because they are knowledgeable about the issue at hand. Gilmore and Campbell (1996) suggest involving 5 to 7 people in the process. The facilitator begins the process by requesting that all participants provide one item of response to the question or problem posed, for example, "What health-risk behaviors are the most problematic in adolescents in this community?" Each person responds in turn and without comment, until all options are indentified and listed for all to consider. Each member of the group is then asked to rank the top 3 to 5 items from the list (Jackson, Pitkin & Kington, 1998). The facilitator tallies the votes, and the group identifies and discusses where they agree and disagree. It should be noted that, after the initial listing of items to consider, discussion may precede ranking. The group then reviews the votes to see if there are clear priorities. If not, those items that can be dropped are eliminated from the process, and the group repeats the ranking and discussion process with those items that are left. When the group agrees on the priority list the process ends.

Data Collection: The Big Picture

There are many forms of data collection. Some are more appropriate in certain situations, environments, and populations than others. Those in charge of conducting the needs assessment should consider the best ways to get the needed information for their particular needs assessment. Despite the particular nature of every needs assessment, the following are some common pieces of advice for the creation of a quality needs assessment:

1. Consider age, literacy levels, first language, accessibility, information needed, and resources when selecting data collection methods.
2. Obtain data in more than one way and from more than one source (triangulation) whenever possible.
3. Identify the process and obtain necessary approvals as early as possible.
4. Pilot-test procedures and instruments.
5. Train your data collectors.
6. Develop a data analysis plan before collecting data.
7. Identify where in the needs assessment or evaluation process you need help and obtain it.
8. There are many ways to collect data. Do your homework in order to identify the best strategies for your situation.

Who to Include in Your Primary Data Collection: Sampling

Because you want to collect information that will help you identify the health needs and assets of a group of people, you want to be sure to get information from everyone in the group, right? Probably not. For small groups, like schools, small worksites, and small health facilities, it may be possible to obtain appropriate information from all students, employees, or clients and the stakeholders. But in most cases, you will have to identify a sample from your group of interest that can provide information that represents the entire group. The size of the group of interest and the amount of resources available for the needs assessment may make it impossible to get data from everyone.

However, beyond issues of resources and decreased cost and time to conduct data collection, there are further advantages to **sampling** the larger group. Using a sample may allow you to increase the scope of your data collection and increase the accuracy of the information collected (Neutens & Rubinson, 2002; Kerlinger, 1986). Getting information from fewer people may allow you to collect a wider range of data or data from a wider range of respondents. Using a sample may improve your response rate (the percentage of those selected to participate that actually participate in the data collection) and decrease errors in data collection, data coding, and data entry. Good response rates and few errors improve the accuracy of the data collected, which improves its ability to represent the real situation.

Probability and nonprobability sampling are both used in needs assessments. Probability sampling is considered to be more accurate in representing the entire group, but nonprobability sampling is generally less expensive and less complicated (Neutens & Rubinson, 2002). Some form of probability sampling should be used whenever possible.

Before you select your sample, you need to clearly identify your sampling frame for each data collection. The sampling frame is a list of all people or items from which the sample is to be taken (Neutens & Robinson, 2002). Existing lists may be used (e.g., student enrollment lists, telephone books, child care centers, employees, and clients) but these will often be incomplete with regard to the true group that needs to be represented. The lists may be out of date or exclude people in some way (e.g., including only those students registered in the current semester or only those people with listed telephone numbers). Effort should be made to add to or combine existing lists and to see whether those not on the list have been excluded in any systematic way that would affect the ability of the list to represent the group of interest. Dee and Jose, working together, could identify a sampling frame for school-age youth in their community. One option would be to use existing public, alternative, and private school enrollment lists, along with lists of those registered as participating in home-schooling.

Checkpoint 7.4

Who would be unintentionally excluded from Dee and Jose's sampling frame list?

Once sampling frames have been determined, sampling techniques must be chosen.

Probability Sampling

In probability sampling, each potential unit (person, address, record) has an equal chance of being selected (Neutens & Rubinson, 2002). Probability techniques include simple random sampling, systematic sampling, stratified random sampling, and cluster sampling.

To conduct a simple random sample, every unit in the sampling frame is assigned a number. Numbers are randomly selected using a random numbers table (Neely, 2003; Neutens & Rubinson, 2002). Selecting a series of people or items based on a predetermined sequence is called systematic sampling. For example, choosing every fifth item on the list would generate a sample of 20% of the total group. For systematic sampling to also be a probability sampling, the original sampling frame list must also be put into random order before the sequential selection is carried out. Systematic sampling may be a good choice for those new to conducting needs assessments, because there is less opportunity for error because of its simplicity (Neutens & Rubinson, 2002).

In a stratified random sample, two or more nonoverlapping subpopulations (strata) are identified, and an independent sample is drawn from each strata. Stratified samples are drawn in order to get a more accurate and nuanced representation of the population or to include characteristics of particular interest (Pedhazer & Schmelkin, 1991). Let us say you were conducting a needs assessment in a relatively culturally heterogenous area and wanted the data to accurately represent the cultural mix. Choosing to conduct a stratified random sample where the strata were racial or ethnic groups would help you to be sure that all groups were adequately represented in the data. Proportional stratified sampling randomly selects a number for each stratum that is proportional to the percentage of that stratum in the entire populations.

Cluster sampling is simple random sampling applied to groups rather than single units. Entire classrooms, worksites, residential blocks, and schools are examples of clusters. Cluster sampling is useful when a list of the population does not exist and when the population is widely scattered geographically (Neutens & Rubinson, 2002). Cluster samples are considered to be less accurate than other forms of simple or stratified random sampling, because the clusters may differ from each other.

Nonprobability Sampling

Nonprobability samples do not represent the entire group from which they are selected. They can only accurately reflect that particular sample. However, they are cheaper and less complicated to use than probability samples (Neutens & Rubinson, 2002). Convenience sampling entails using a group that is easy to access. Surveying your health classes to get a sense of the health-risk behaviors of the high school students in your community is an example. The information you obtain will only represent the behaviors of those students in your class, but it will be convenient for you to collect and will give you some information about potential health-risk behavior problems in your larger target group. Using only those who volunteer to provide information is another form of nonprobability sampling. Volunteers do not represent the larger population for the simple reason that only some volunteered and others did not. Volunteer samples are generally put together by asking people to fill out a survey or be interviewed. Flyers, newspaper or television advertisements, and radio spots may alert people to the need and supply participation details. Information from those who volunteer, rather than those who are selected, can be useful as long as it is understood that, as a group, the volunteers are different from the general target population.

In purposive sampling, those conducting the needs assessment think about who might be the best people to provide information for the purposes of the needs assessment (Neutens & Rubinson, 2002). Brainstorming a potential list of key informants and then determining who would be best to interview is an example of purposive sampling.

Snowball sampling is another form of nonprobability sampling. In snowball sampling, people or respondents are identified who can refer those conducting the needs assessment to other potential respondents (Atkinson & Flint, n.d.). This technique can be especially useful in accessing hard to reach groups.

Jose and Dee have worked with the data collection working groups and have received input from the coalition and advisory board in order to create a data collection plan.

Summary

Needs assessment and evaluation plans should strive to identify necessary and appropriate primary and secondary, quantitative and qualitative data. Those planning data collection activities must consider the resources available for data collection (time, people, and money) and the characteristics of the target population. A variety of data collection activities should be used.

QUESTIONS

1. What are the advantages and disadvantages of using interview techniques to collect data?
2. What should you look for when selecting an instrument for use in data collection?
3. What are the benefits of sampling?
4. What are the advantages and disadvantages of using electronic surveys versus telephone surveys?
5. When might it be appropriate and beneficial to use group consensus techniques?

EXERCISES

1. Find the latest US Census data for your county. Select three or four pieces of data. Select two or three places in the county that may have

more up-to-date information. Phone or visit these locations to get the more recent data. How do they compare?

2. You want to collect eating behavior information about preschool youth, elementary school-age youth, adolescents, and young adults. Consider the characteristics of these groups and decide how and where you might collect this information from each of these groups? Go to the professional literature and look at documents describing projects that have collected information on the eating behaviors of these groups. Compare the actions described in the documents to what you suggested.

3. Locate a survey that is commonly used to measure youth or adult health behaviors. Use professional sources to find the reading level of the survey, the directions for administering the survey, and at least one study that used the survey in a needs assessment.

4. Ask five of your friends to answer, in writing, the following: "Do you consider your quality of life high, medium, or low? Why? Explain." Take their responses and read them over. Are there any common themes in their responses? What key words jump out at you when you read them? Attempt to create a group summary response.

5. Locate a needs assessment that was completed by a local agency or organization. Read through the document. Looking at the data, do you agree with the priorities and conclusions in the document? Write a memo to the agency outlining the priorities you see based on the data.

REFERENCES

Atkinson, R. & Flint, J. (n.d.). Accessing hidden and hard-to-reach populations: Snowball research strategies. *Social Research Update, 33.* Retrieved March 1, 2003, from http://www.soc.surrey.ac.uk/sru/SRU33.html.

Duffield, C. (1993). The Delphi technique: A comparison of results obtained using two expert panels. *International Journal of Nursing Studies, 30,* 227–237.

Eng, E. & Blanchard, L. (1990). Action-oriented community diagnosis: A health education tool. *International Journal of Community Health Education, 11*(2), 93–100.

Gilmore, G. D. & Campbell, M. D. (1996). *Needs assessment strategies for health education and health promotion* (pp. 65–72). Dubuque, IA: Brown and Benchmark.

Goldman, K. D. & Schmalz, K. J. (2001). Focus on focus groups! *Health promotion practice, 2*(1), 14–15.

Goldman, K. D. & Schmalz, K. J. (2000). Reading an article between the lines. *Health Promotion Practice, 1*(4), 300–306.

Goslin, N. (n.d.). *What is photo novella: The C. J. Peete youth club photo novella program.* Retrieved March 1, 2003, from http://www.tulane.edu/~cjpeete/pictures/Photo%20Novella/pictures.html/.

Hodges, B. C., Videto, D. M. & Gefell, T. (2001) *Moving marathon: The success of a healthy heart coalition.* Paper presented at the SOPHE Annual Meeting, Atlanta, GA.

Hodges, B. C. (1992). *Development of an instrument to measure perceived health risk and perceived health education needs of middle school students.* Unpublished doctoral dissertation, University of Maryland, College Park, MD.

Isaac, S. & Michael, W. (1981). *Handbook in research and evaluation* (2nd ed.). San Diego, CA: Edits.

Jackson, C. A., Pitkin, K. & Kington, R. (1998). *Evidence-based decision-making for community health programs.* (MR-933-MLHS). Santa Monica, CA: RAND. Retrieved February 28, 2003, from http:// www.rand.org/publications/electronic/health.html.

Kerlinger, F. N. (1986). *Foundations of behavioral research* (3rd ed.). Fort Worth, TX: Holt, Rinehart and Winston.

Neutens, J. J. & Rubinson, L. (2002). *Research techniques for the health sciences* (3rd ed.). San Francisco: Benjamin Cummings.

Pedhazer, E. J. & Schmelkin, L. (1991). *Measurement, design, and analysis: An integrated approach.* Mahwah, NJ: Lawrence Erlbaum Associates.

Selwyn, N. & Robson, K. (1998). Using e-mail as a research tool. *Social Research Update, 21.* Retrieved March 1, 2003, from http://www.soc.surrey.ac.uk/sru/SRU21.html.

Sharpe, P. A., Greany, M. L., Lee, P. R. & Royce, S. W. (2000). Assets-oriented community assessment. *Public Health Reports, 113,* 205–211.

Thomas, S. B. & Hodges, B. C. (1991). Assessing AIDS knowledge, attitudes, and risk behaviors among black and Hispanic homosexual and bisexual men. *Journal of Sex Education and Therapy, 17*(2), 116–124.

Thompson, N. J. & McClintock, H. O. (1998). *Demonstrating your program's worth: A primer on evaluation for programs to prevent unintentional injury.* Atlanta, GA: Centers for Disease Control and Prevention, National Center for Injury Prevention and Control.

Tilson, E. C., McBride, C. M., Albright, J. B. & Sargent, J. D. (2001). Attitudes towards smoking and family-based health promotion among rural mothers and other primary caregivers who smoke. *The Journal of School Health, 71*(10), 489–494.

Torabi, M. R. & Ding, K. (1998). Selected critical measurement and statistical issues in health education evaluation and research. *The International Electronic Journal of Health Education, 1*(1), 26–38.

Wang, C. & Burris, M. A. (1994). Empowerment through photo novella: Portraits of participation. *Health Education Quarterly, 21*(2), 171–186.

World Health Organization [WHO] (2000). *Reproductive health during conflict and displacement: A guide for programme managers.* Geneva: Switzerland: World

Health Organization. Retrieved November 12, 2002, from http://www.who.int/re-productivehealth/publications/RHR_00_13_RH_conflict_and_displacement/PDF_RHR_00_13/chapter10.en.pdf.

Ziglio, E. (1996). The Delphi method and its contribution to decision-making. In Adler, M. & Ziglio, E. (eds.), *Gazing into the oracle: The Delphi method and its application to social policy and public health* (pp. 3–33). London: Jessica Kingsley.

8

Program Evaluation: Background and Basics

Key Terms: *formative evaluation, summative evaluation, process evaluation, impact evaluation, outcome evaluation, efficiency evaluation*

> Jose's funders are requiring him to evaluate programs that were developed with their monies to see if the programs are meeting their objectives. Dee is very interested in seeing whether the pieces of the program for grades K–12 will actually be implemented as they are intended. Many of the community members who have been working on program planning are excited about the various activities and want to see if the participants like the programs as much as they do. Dee and Jose realize that it is time to begin to outline an evaluation plan.

There is a growing need for well-designed and widely disseminated program evaluations in health education and health promotion (Rimer, Glanz & Rasband, 2001). The increasing focus on the use of evidence-based programs and curricula; the need to contribute to the scientific base of health education and health promotion in order to support the profession; and the need to *improve* programs as well as measure their outcomes requires that those working in health promotion and health education have a grounding in program evaluation.

Most people understand that program evaluation is done, in part, to see if a program is doing what it was intended to do—meeting its goals and objectives. However, there are many reasons to conduct an evaluation. Windsor, Baranowski, Clark, and Cutter (1994) outline these reasons to conduct evaluations of health education programs:

- To see if program objectives were met

- To note the strengths and weaknesses of the program to assist in making decisions about the program and its parts
- To monitor progress toward program goals and objectives
- To provide information to determine the program's cost-efficiency and cost-effectiveness
- To improve staff skills in planning, implementing, and evaluating activities
- To fulfill requirements of funding sources
- To show the effectiveness of the program to the target population, public, stakeholders, funding agencies, and those who may want to implement similar programs (Handler, 2002; Thompson & McClintock, 2000)
- To determine generalizability of the program to other populations or settings
- To contribute to health education knowledge on program design
- To generate hypotheses about health behavior for future research

Thompson and McClintock (2000) also point out that evaluations can help determine if program materials are appropriate, can help managers improve service, and can serve as an early-warning system for potentially serious problems with the program. The W. K. Kellogg Foundation (1998, p. 8) adds that conducting evaluation activities can serve to improve and increase the "skills, knowledge, and perspectives" of those involved in the evaluation, thus building the capacity of the institution or organization to continue the program and the evaluation processes.

After reviewing the above list, it becomes apparent that evaluation is not an action that happens once at the end of a program. Evaluation is an ongoing process that produces information used by a variety of people to describe, improve, adapt, and make decisions about programs.

Types of Evaluation

There are a variety of types of program evaluations that one can conduct. Although the evaluation literature sometimes varies in its uses of the evaluation terms, in health education and health promotion, they are generally defined in the following manner:

Formative Evaluation

Formative evaluation is a broad term referring to an evaluation that is conducted for the purpose of getting information to be used to improve a program. Formative evaluation may occur during program planning or implementation. During program planning, formative evaluation activities test program plans, messages, materials, procedures, modifications of existing programs or materials *before* they are implemented to verify the feasibility, appropriateness, and acceptability of their use in the program and with the target populations (CDC, 2002). Pilot-testing and process evaluation activities are part of formative evaluation. Formative evaluation activities are also completed *after* implementation to identify the source and solution of unanticipated problems that arise after a program has been implemented.

Summative Evaluation

Summative evaluation is a broad term referring to an evaluation that is conducted for the purpose of determining whether a program worked (Bartholomew et al., 2001). Its focus is on describing what happened and whether the program produced its intended effects, rather than on providing information for program improvement.

Process Evaluation

The purpose of **process evaluation** is to monitor and document organizational and program-related factors in order to improve the effectiveness of the program, provide support for maintaining the program, help explain why goals and objectives may or may not have been attained, and to help make decisions about the program and its components (W. K. Kellogg Foundation, 1998, p. 25). Essentially, process evaluation data allow program planners and evaluators to explain why a program may or may not have been effective. It may occur as part of a formative evaluation, as in a pilot test, or as part of a summative evaluation, as the program is implemented (Bartholomew et al., 2001).

Process evaluation includes the assessment of several areas. One of these areas, often referred to as implementation evaluation, measures and documents whether all program elements were implemented or implemented as intended (CSAP 2002a; Bartholomew et al., 2001; Thompson & McClintock, 2000; W. K. Kellogg Foundation, 1998; CDC, 1997; Windsor et al., 1994). How close did the implementation come to what was planned? Is the program reaching the intended target population and how many members of the target population are being reached (USDA, 2003; CSAP, 2002a; CDC, 2002)? What barriers were encountered while implementing the program and its components (W. K. Kellogg Foundation, 1998)? These are questions that are investigated in implementation evaluation.

Charting progress towards stated program goals and program objectives is another part of process evaluation. Measuring intermediate, day-to-day objectives associated with each program component helps identify potential problems with the program or its implementation early on so that they may be adjusted (Deeds, 2000; Green & Kreuter, 1999; W. K. Kellogg Foundation, 1998).

Perceptions and satisfaction levels are other areas investigated as part of process evaluation (W. K. Kellogg Foundation, 1998). What are community members' perceptions of the program? Is the target or client population satisfied with the program and its activities? To what degree are they satisfied? Assessing staff performance, staff satisfaction with the program, and staff perceptions of the program are also included in process evaluation (USDA, 2003; CSAP, 2002a; CDC, 2002).

A resource review may also be conducted as part of the process evaluation. This can include a budget review (Windsor et al., 1994), an assessment of whether the staff was adequately trained, and an assessment of whether sufficient time to implement and conduct program activities was allotted (W. K. Kellogg Foundation, 1998).

Impact Evaluation

Impact evaluation is the measurement of the extent to which the program has caused the intended short-term changes in the target population (CDC, 2002; Green & Kreuter, 1999; CDC, 1997). Changes in the program's short-term program goals and objectives are assessed. Depending on the nature of the goals and objectives, impact evaluation looks at improvement in behavioral, environmental, predisposing, reinforcing, and enabling factors.

Outcome Evaluation

An **outcome evaluation** focuses on whether the long-term goals of the program were attained. Changes in health status or quality of life indices are measured (Green & Kreuter, 1999). It is also important to attempt to measure any unintended outcomes that arise as a result of the program and the program's impact on related organizations and institutions (W. K. Kellogg Foundation, 1998).

Efficiency Evaluation

An **efficiency evaluation** looks at the costs of the program in relation to its effects (CSAP, 2002a; Batholomew et al., 2001).

Conducting an Evaluation

A program evaluation is an ongoing process that begins during program development. There are actions common to conducting any evaluation. A useful way to think about these common actions is presented by the Center for Substance Abuse Prevention (CSAP) (2002a, p. 4). The CSAP has organized the common actions into eight steps:

1. Conceptualize the evaluation
2. Design the evaluation
3. Hire and train the evaluation staff

4. Choose and test the instruments and procedures

5. Collect evaluation data

6. Analyze and report data

7. Make changes to your program based on the data

8. Evaluate again

Each of these steps is briefly discussed.

Step 1: Conceptualize the Evaluation

Evaluation planning should begin as the program is being planned (Bartholomew et al., 2001; Thompson & McClintock, 2000; Green & Kreuter, 1999). One of the first tasks to be addressed is a discussion of who will conduct your program evaluation (Thompson & McClintock, 2000). Ideally, the evaluation should be planned and conducted by a team consisting of an evaluation director, relevant stakeholders, and relevant staff (W. K. Kellogg Foundation, 1998). This structure will help to ensure that the evaluation is responsive to the needs of all constituencies. This is especially important when working with marginalized or underrepresented groups (W. K. Kellogg Foundation, 1998, p. 68).

Are there people on the staff with expertise in program evaluation that could be placed in charge? Does the funding source require an outside evaluator? Sometimes, program planning staff are so invested in the program, it is difficult for them to be objective in an evaluation. Box 8.1 contains a list of suggested criteria for outside evaluators.

Whether you are using internal or outside evaluators (or both) it is essential to the evaluation planning process to be able to clearly describe the program, its components, its intended effects, and how those intended effects are produced (CSAP, 2002a; Bartholomew et al., 2001). Developing one or more logic models is suggested (W. K. Kellogg Foundation, 1998). These logic models graphically represent the program components, intended outcomes (Figure 8.1), and the theoretical constructs underlying the program. The outcomes model depicts the interrelationships among the program objectives and program goals, clearly illustrating which shorter-term objectives need to be achieved in order to lead to specific long-term goals. The emphasis, however, is on identifying the shorter-term, intermediate objectives so that they can be measured (W. K. Kellogg Foundation, 1998, p. 36). The activities logic model illustrates the links among program activities and identifies their temporal relationship (Figure 8.2). An activities logic model is useful when looking at the implementation of the program, as it allows the evaluators to note if the program has been implemented at all or in the desired order, and to note where any barriers to implementation may have occurred. A theory logic

---

Box 8.1   Outside evaluator criteria.

- Has background and experience in conducting evaluations of programs like yours
- Has knowledge of a variety of evaluation techniques or techniques in the specific area with which you need assistance
- Is familiar with and understands the goals and values of the school, community, or site in which the evaluation will be conducted
- Is familiar with a variety of instruments and data collection techniques so that the best match can be made between the data collection process and the population involved in the evaluation (e.g., regarding language or age)
- Is aware of the current theories and models associated with the goals and objectives of your program and has a clear concept of the conceptual framework of the program
- Is affordable within the program and evaluation budget
- Is available and accessible and able to troubleshoot when unexpected glitches happen (data collection snafus)
- Has good communication skills (can talk to staff and program participants in layman's terms, is approachable, etc.)

Source: Center for Substance Abuse Prevention, Substance Abuse and Mental Health Services Administration, Department of Health and Human Services (2002). *CSAP's prevention pathways: Evaluation for the unevaluated: Evaluation 101.* Retrieved July 1, 2003, from http://pathwayscourses.samhsa.gov/samhsa_pathways/courses/eval101_supps_pg1.htm.

---

model represents how the program is expected or assumed to work by graphically linking together the underlying theoretical constructs of the program. Bartholomew and colleagues (2001) recommend that two evaluation logic maps be created, a process map and an impact map. The process map describes the organization of the program and the intended interaction of the target population with the program or service. The impact map depicts how the program intervention activities result in intended outcomes. Creating the logic models while planning the program will not only help develop a program based on sound logic and theory, but will serve as the basis for the evaluation plan.

Step 2: Design the Evaluation

Designing the evaluation involves planning the details of your evaluation (Figure 8.3). This step begins by determining specifically what program planners, clients and participants, stakeholders, funders, and other important constituencies want to evaluate.

Many find it helpful to think of evaluation as answering a set of questions about the program. Thus, at this point, those conducting the evaluation should identify all the questions that they and significant others may want answered about the program. Examples of questions that might be asked for each type

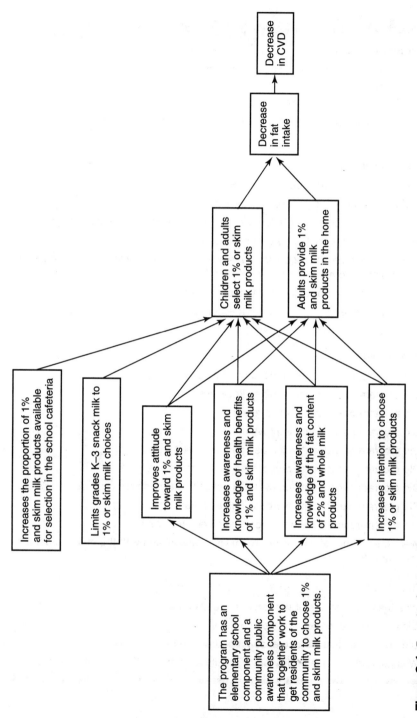

Figure 8.1 Example of an impact map.

Box 8.2   Examples of general evaluation questions.

Formative Evaluation

Are the written materials used at an appropriate reading level for the target population?

Are the videotapes acceptable to the target population?

Are the workshops offered at a time that is convenient for the target population?

Process Evaluation

Was the program implemented as planned?

Did all sessions or components occur? If not, why not?

Did sessions or components last as long as they were supposed to last?

Were components facilitated by those trained?

How many people attended each session? How many people participated in all or parts of the program?

What was the level of student satisfaction with the unit?

What was the level of facilitator or teacher satisfaction with the intervention or unit?

Impact Evaluation

Did the program meet its short-term goals and objectives?

Did program participants increase knowledge?

Did program participants improve skills?

Did program participants improve self-efficacy?

Did program participants increase perceived susceptibility?

Did program participants reduce health-compromising behavior?

Did program participants delay the onset of health-compromising behavior?

Did program participants increase health-enhancing behavior?

Did the environment become more health-enhancing?

Were the number of emergency room visits associated with the health problem decreased?

Outcome Evaluation

Was the health status of the target population improved?

Did CVD rates decrease for the community?

Did playground injuries decrease for county day care centers?

Was the quality of life of the target population improved?

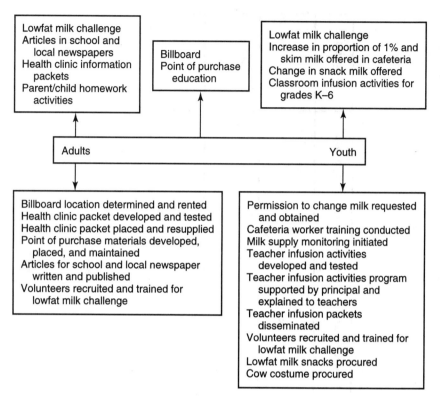

Figure 8.2 Example of a logic model.

of evaluation can be found in Box 8.2. Evaluation design will be discussed further in the next chapter.

Step 3: Hire and Train the Evaluation Staff

Those designing and directing the evaluation will need to determine if additional staff are required to conduct the evaluation activities. If so, these people will have to be identified and hired. All those involved in the evaluation activities will have to be trained to conduct the activities in which they will be involved. Evaluation activities that often require additional staff and training include data collection, data coding, data cleaning, data entry, and data analysis (CSAP, 2002a).

Step 4: Choose and Test the Instruments and Procedures

The evaluation team should begin by reviewing the evaluation questions that have been selected. The team must then determine what information is required in order to answer each question, from whom or where this information may be obtained, and when the information should and can be collected.

Evaluation question	Information needed	From whom	How collected	When collected	Type data	Analysis

Figure 8.3 Example of a planning table for planning evaluation data collection procedures.

The CSAP (2002b) provides a useful list of questions for the evaluation team to answer as it is selecting data collection procedures.

1. What sources are likely to provide the most accurate information?
2. What sources are the least costly or time consuming?
3. Does the information collection process pose an undue burden on the sources? Consider what respondents can realistically do in the way of filling out surveys, keeping logs, talking with people and the like (W. K. Kellogg Foundation, 1998).
4. Who will administer the instruments?
5. Where will they be administered?
6. How long does it take to administer the instrument?
7. How will the instruments be collected (e.g., passed in tear-off sheet, mailed, hand delivered in a sealed envelope)?
8. How many copies do you need of completed instruments?
9. Where will the original completed instruments be kept?

The time constraints of respondents, sensitivity to cultural issues in the community or target population, reading levels, language and communication issues, and the importance of the information to the overall evaluation need to be considered when answering these questions (W. K. Kellogg Foundation, 1998). A mix of methods and procedures will provide a stronger evaluation.

As discussed in Chapter 7, it is usually most beneficial to locate and use existing data collection tools, especially surveys and interview questionnaires. Using existing measures may ensure an established level of reliability and validity, makes it easier to compare your evaluation results to others that have used the same measurement tools (CSAP, 2002b), and saves time.

Step 5: Collect Evaluation Data

Evaluation data should be collected as determined by the evaluation plan and time-line developed during the design step. It is important to train all data collectors.

Step 6: Analyze and Report Data

Data analysis should be performed as outlined in the evaluation plan. Once data have been analyzed, the results can be interpreted in relation to the evaluation questions by the evaluation team. Evaluation results are then communicated to stakeholders, participants, funders, other program planners, and all others with an interest in the program.

Those that advocate for and support the participation of target population members and others in the analysis of the evaluation data suggest developing short video or audio presentations of the results for discussion and analysis activities, or for staging debates, in which opposing points of view about the results can be presented (W. K. Kellogg Foundation, 1998).

Evaluators should prepare at least three kinds of reports (CSAP, 2003b). An executive summary briefly outlines the evaluation, its major findings, and recommendations for the program. It is useful to prepare several different executive summaries and less jargonistic articles in order to quickly communicate the major findings of the evaluation to different audiences (W. K. Kellogg Foundation, 1998).

A research report provides a detailed description of all evaluation activities, findings, conclusions, recommendations, and insights. A replication manual is often prepared so that others can implement the program.

There are several other ways to consider for communicating the evaluation findings and recommendations. Those in charge of the program and the evaluation can prepare press releases and disseminate them to local media outlets. Holding a press conference to release the findings of the evaluation can also be effective. Others advocate giving verbal presentations to select groups to get the word out (W. K. Kellogg Foundation, 1998). A program or project Web site on which evaluation data, results, and recommendations are posted may also be used as a way to communicate with a variety of constituencies.

Checkpoint 8.1

List at least three different audiences for an evaluation executive summary. How should the summary differ for each audience?

Regardless of the methods used for communicating results, conclusions, and recommendations, data should be presented graphically in ways that summarize and illustrate. Colorful and easy-to-read charts, graphs, and pictures must be included in all materials used to communicate the findings.

Step 7: Make Changes to Your Program Based on the Data

Program planners and program staff should work together to improve the program based upon the evaluation findings and recommendations (CSAP, 2002a).

Step 8: Evaluate Again

Evaluation should be ongoing. Continue to monitor program processes, results, and improvements.

Evaluation Principles

The American Evaluation Association has developed a set of five guiding principles for evaluators (Newman et al., 1998, pp. 1–2), which are designed to apply to all kinds of evaluations. Although intended for professional evaluators, they are useful and important for those who conduct evaluations as only part of what they do and for those considering hiring professional evaluators. The principles are as follows:

- Systematic inquiry: Evaluators engage in evaluation design and carry out systematic, data-based evaluation activities.
- Competence: Evaluators provide competent performance to stakeholders.
- Integrity and honesty: Evaluators ensure the honesty and integrity of the entire evaluation process.
- Respect for people: Evaluators respect the security, dignity, and self-worth of the respondents, program participants, clients, and other stakeholders with whom they interact.
- Responsibilities for general and public welfare: Evaluators articulate and take into account the diversity of interests and values that may be related to the general and public welfare.

Summary

Program evaluation is a vital part of the program planning process and should be designed so that it illustrates what a program is doing, how the program can be improved, and whether the program is meeting its goals and objectives. An evaluation plan should include a combination of a variety of different activities that are ethical, feasible, and provide accurate data. The evaluation activities and resulting information should be meaningful and useful to program planners, program staff, and the target population.

> The program planning groups have each mapped out how their program pieces relate to the overall goals and objectives of the coalition. Dee and Jose have collected some evaluation questions that a variety of people want answered. However, they realize that they are going to need some help in evaluating their efforts.

QUESTIONS

1. What are the differences between formative and summative evaluations?
2. What are the differences between process, impact, and outcome evaluations?
3. How do process, impact, and outcome evaluations relate to the Precede portion of the Precede–Proceed model?

4. What are the five guiding principles for evaluators?

5. What are the eight steps of the evaluation process?

EXERCISES

1. Locate an article in a professional journal that describes an evaluation of a health-related program. Write a one-page summary of the evaluation article, identifying which type(s) of evaluation were conducted. Share it with your classmates.

2. You want to evaluate whether a new curriculum will improve attitudes and behaviors in your middle school more than the existing one. Conceptualize this evaluation. What evaluation approaches would be used? Who would you want on your evaluation planning team? Support your responses.

3. Research how school health and community health education training programs at colleges and universities are evaluated for the purposes of accreditation. How do these evaluations differ from those used for the accreditation of the college or university health center?

4. Make an appointment with the head of your local health department to discuss how decisions are made about which programs to evaluate and how to evaluate them.

5. Volunteer to assist a local health organization or agency with evaluation-related data collection. Share your experiences with the class.

REFERENCES

Bartholomew, L. K., Parcel, G. S., Kok, G. & Gottlieb, N. H. (2001). *Intervention mapping*. Mountain View, CA: Mayfield.

Centers for Disease Control and Prevention [CDC] (March 2002). *Evaluation guidance handbook: Strategies for implementing the evaluation guidance for CDC-funded HIV prevention programs*. Atlanta, GA: Centers for Disease Control and Prevention.

Centers for Disease Control and Prevention [CDC] (1997). *Coordinated school health program infrastructure development: Process evaluation manual*. Atlanta, GA: US Department of Health and Human Services, Centers for Disease Control and Prevention.

Center for Substance Abuse Prevention [CSAP], Substance Abuse and Mental Health Services Administration, US Department of Health and Human Services (2002a). *CSAP's prevention pathways: Evaluation for the unevaluated: Evaluation*

101. Retrieved July 1, 2003, from http://pathwayscourses.samhsa.gov/samhsa_pathways/courses/eval101_toc.htm.

Center for Substance Abuse Prevention [CSAP], Substance Abuse and Mental Health Services Administration, Department of Health and Human Services (2002b). *CSAP's prevention pathways: Evaluation for the unevaluated: Evaluation 101.* Retrieved July 1, 2003, from http://pathwayscourses.samhsa.gov/samhsa_pathways/courses/eval101_2_pg8.htm.

Deeds, S. G. (2000). *The health education specialist: A study guide for professional competence.* Allentown, PA: National Commission for Health Education Credentialing.

Green, L. W. & Kreuter, M. W. (1999). *Health promotion planning: An educational and ecological approach* (3rd ed.). Mountain View, CA: Mayfield.

Handler, A. (2002). Role of evaluation in policy development and implementation. Retrieved July 20, 2003, from http://www.uic.edu/sph/mch/evaluation/evaluation/class/.

Newman, D., Scheirer, M. A., Shadish, W. & Wye, C. (1998). Guiding principles for evaluators: A report from the AEA task force on guiding principles for evaluators. *Practical Assessment, Research, and Evaluation.* Retrieved August 15, 2003, from http://erica,net/pare/getvn.asp?=6&n=3.

Rimer, B. K., Glanz, K. & Rasband, G. (2001). Searching for evidence about health education and health behavior interventions. *Health Education and Behavior, 28*(3), 231–248.

Thompson, N. J. & McClintock, H. O. (2000). *Demonstrating your program's worth: A primer on evaluation for programs to prevent unintentional injury* (2nd ed.). Atlanta, GA: Centers for Disease Control and Prevention; National Center for Injury Prevention and Control.

US Department of Agriculture [USDA] (2003). *Program evaluation.* Washington, DC: US Department of Agriculture, Food Safety and Inspection Service, Office of Policy, Program Development, and Evaluation. Retrieved on July 15, 2003, from http://www.fsis.usda.gov/oppde/peis/Evaluation/Types.htm.

Windsor, R., Baranowski, T., Clark, N. & Cutter, G. (1994). *Evaluation of health promotion, health education, and disease prevention programs* (2nd ed.). Mountain View, CA: Mayfield.

W. K. Kellogg Foundation (1998). *Evaluation handbook.* Battle Creek, MI: Collateral Management.

9

Evaluation Structure and Design

Key Terms: *objectives-oriented, management-oriented, consumer-oriented, expertise-oriented, adversary-oriented, naturalistic-oriented, CIPP Model, experimental design, quasi-experimental design, internal validity, external validity, history, maturation, testing, instrumentation, selection, experimental mortality, contamination, Hawthorne effect, expectancy effect, novelty and disruption effects, social desirability.*

> The coalition has pooled its resources to hire an evaluation consultant to help the group design evaluations of its programs. A new evaluation workgroup has been formed that includes a representative from the local college, coalition steering committee members, Dee, Jose, and the consultant. This workgroup began meeting with program planners occasionally at the beginning of the program planning process and is now ready to finalize its evaluation design.

Just as there are a variety of reasons to conduct a program evaluation, there are a variety of approaches to conducting a program evaluation. In most cases, an eclectic combination of approaches, constructed by picking and choosing from the approaches that are most consistent with the evaluation needs that have been identified, will result in an evaluation that is useful to all. Worthen and Sanders (1987) classify the various evaluation approaches into six categories.

Objectives-oriented approaches are focused on the outcomes of the program. Evaluators can focus on measuring the attainment of stated objectives or measuring actual outcomes. It is useful to keep in mind that the outcomes being assessed may have been stated ahead of time or may be unexpected. The goal-free approach (Scriven, 1972) to evaluation looks at what has resulted from the program, whether or not the outcomes were previously expected or stated in objectives.

Management-oriented approaches are used when the evaluation needs to assist administrators in making decisions about the program. Evaluators determine with administrators what decisions need to be made and then collect data that will be used by the administrators in making fair decisions based on clearly delineated criteria. Stufflebeam's **CIPP Model** (1973, 2002) includes process, impact, effectiveness, sustainability, transportability, and meta-evaluation components. Process evaluation, in this context, focuses on evaluation activities to manage and document progress through the program, monitor program costs, and strengthen program components. Impact and effectiveness evaluations, respectively, look at whether the program is reaching the target populations and achieving the program's positive and negative outcomes related to the target population and the community in general. These are conducted in order to make a "bottom line assessment of the program's success" (Stufflebeam, 2002, p. 9). Transportability evaluation determines how easily the program has been adapted or could be adapted in other situations. Meta-evaluation assesses the degree to which the evaluation was in accordance with sound evaluation standards.

Consumer-oriented approaches are designed to provide an evaluation of products and programs based on a set of criteria developed and applied by individuals, groups, or organizations that are independent of the program being looked at. Applying the same set of criteria to similar programs and services, and then disseminating the findings, allows potential consumers of the product or service to make informed decisions. Checklists with rating scales and the application of rubrics are often used.

Expertise-oriented approaches use the subjective assessment of relevant professional experts to provide feedback and judgement. Evaluation activities associated with professional accreditation and licensing are an example of this approach.

Adversary-oriented approaches employ evaluation activities that actively seek to elicit opposing viewpoints within the evaluation framework. These approaches are concerned with making sure that the evaluation is as unbiased as possible and includes discussion and presentation of both the strengths and weaknesses of the program.

Naturalistic-oriented and participant-oriented approaches view the involvement of the program's participants and clients in the evaluation process as paramount. The evaluation is designed to provide a broad description of the program and its outcomes from multiple perspectives using a variety of types of data. It can often provide evaluation planners with innovative ways to answer evaluation

Checkpoint 9.1

Why would it be important to include a variety of approaches in your program evaluation?

questions that are acceptable to the evaluation participants, and it also fosters ownership of the program (Springett, 2003).

Designing the Evaluation

Although research techniques are used to conduct evaluations, evaluation and research differ. Research is designed to be objective and "value-free" whereas evaluation, by its very nature, attempts to determine the value of a program (Springett, 2003). Whose values determine program worth, and against what objective standards will the program be judged are issues that evaluators must address. Springett (2003) points out that for health education and health promotion programs, which are multidisciplinary in nature, the values by which a program can be judged are often at odds. Thus, the evaluation design should be driven by developing the best ways in which to answer the evaluation questions selected, rather than by any particular design or approach.

As mentioned in the previous chapter, the first steps in designing the evaluation are to review the resources available for evaluation purposes and to generate evaluation questions. Ideally, evaluation questions should be elicited from all relevant constituencies: target population, stakeholders, program staff and volunteers, participants, and funders. The evaluation questions are then prioritized, based on a mutually acceptable set of criteria, and then chosen in a systematic manner.

Those responsible for conducting the evaluation should consider each question and how it can best be answered. Data needed to answer each question should come from multiple sources whenever possible and include both qualitative and quantitative data types. Chapter 7 reviews data collection techniques.

When conducting impact and outcome evaluations, evaluation planners must consider internal validity and external validity (Cook & Campbell, 1979) when deciding how to answer each question. **Internal validity** is the concept of the level of confidence in being able to say it was the program that caused any changes. Minimizing outside influences beyond the program that could affect the desired program outcomes increases internal validity. **External validity** is the concept of identifying those to whom we can apply the results of the evaluation. It is a function of who is involved in the evaluation study and the characteristics of environment of the evaluation (e.g., exact procedures, testing effects, and types of measurement). High internal validity results in low external validity and vice versa. Tight control of outside influences is difficult in evaluations conducted in the "real world," as are many health education and health promotion program evaluations (Neutens & Rubinson, 2002). The evaluation plan must find a balance between the two that makes sense for the situation, the stakeholders, and the target population. This can be accomplished by considering threats to both internal and external validity when selecting evaluation designs and procedures. These threats are discussed at the end of the chapter.

Experimental and Quasi-experimental Designs in Evaluation

Experimental designs result in the strongest evidence of the effectiveness of a program by minimizing threats to internal validity (Neutens & Rubinson, 2002; Thompson & McClintock, 1998). They are based on the random assignment of participants into one or more groups and the measurement of both groups. The randomization of evaluation participants allows evaluators to assume that important traits that might affect the measurement of the program's outcomes (e.g., age, gender, some personality traits, and maturation levels) have been equally distributed among the groups (Neutens & Rubinson, 2002). However, experimental designs require that potential evaluation participants agree to being randomly assigned, require a relatively large number of participants, delay program participation for the control group (Neutens & Rubinson, 2002), and generally cost more than other designs (Thompson & McClintock, 1998). These challenges decrease the generalizability of results from evaluations using these designs.

Quasi-experimental designs reduce threats to validity but cannot control for all threats to validity. These designs compare two or more groups, but do not require random assignment (Neutens & Rubinson, 2002; Thompson & McClintock, 1998). These designs are commonly used in health education and health promotion evaluations, because they can provide evaluation data that can be supported with some degree of confidence and are more realistic for use in real-world situations. Quasi-experimental designs often use intact groups, such as classrooms, school districts, worksites, clinic populations, and volunteers, as participants in the evaluation. Evaluators choosing these designs must select comparison groups carefully so that they are as similar as possible.

A review of experimental and quasi-experimental designs follows. A schematic of each design presented accompanies a brief discussion. In the schematic, R indicates randomization, X indicates the intervention or program, M indicates a measurement, and M^1, M^2, M^3, and so on indicate first measurement, second measurement, third measurement, and so on. The experimental group is the group that receives the intervention. The different groups involved in the evaluation are placed on different lines.

Experimental Designs

In experimental designs, two or more "equivalent" groups are compared on the predetermined outcomes. One or more groups receive the new program and one or more groups do not receive any program or receive the existing program.

Those identified or recruited to be evaluation participants are randomly assigned into one group. Random assignment can be carried out using a computer program, a table of random numbers, or, if only two groups are used, a toss of a coin.

Posttest-Only Control Group

$$R \qquad X \qquad M$$
$$R \qquad \qquad M$$

The strengths of this design include the lack of a pretest effect. It is a good choice when pretests are inappropriate or unavailable. However, this design cannot determine if change occurred from before the program to after the program. It only allows evaluators to determine if those that receive the intervention are different on the outcome measures than those that did not receive the intervention.

Pretest–Posttest Control Group

$$R \qquad M \qquad X \qquad M$$
$$R \qquad M \qquad \qquad M$$

The pretests in this design are given to ensure the equivalence of the two groups before the program is given to the experimental group. Pretest data are analyzed to see whether the experimental and control groups are similar or different.

Time Series

$$R \qquad M^1\, M^2\, M^3\, M^4 \qquad X \qquad M^1\, M^2\, M^3\, M^4$$
$$R \qquad M^1\, M^2\, M^3\, M^4 \qquad \qquad M^1\, M^2\, M^3\, M^4$$

A time series design can be used to look at other factors beyond those in the program that might contribute to differences found between experimental and contol groups. Time series designs allow evaluators to somewhat address the possibility of maturation threats within groups by looking at trends, rather than single points in time. However, data collection errors may increase.

Pretest Posttest Follow-up

$$R \qquad M^1 \qquad X \qquad M^1\, M^2\, M^3\, M^4$$
$$R \qquad M^1 \qquad \qquad M^1\, M^2\, M^3\, M^4$$

Although time series designs can be used to look at the maintenance of program effects, multiple pretests are not always feasible or desirable. This design, using multiple posttests, requires fewer resources.

Crossover Design

$$R \qquad M^1 \qquad X \qquad M^2\, M^3\, M^4 \qquad\qquad M^5\, M^6\, M^7$$
$$R \qquad M^1 \qquad\qquad M^2\, M^3\, M^4 \qquad X \qquad M^5\, M^6\, M^7$$

Crossover designs are selected when all those eligible to participate in a program must receive the intervention (Thompson & McClintock, 1998, p. 59). Participants are randomly assigned into two groups, and both groups receive a pretest in order to verify the outcomes of interest as mandated by the evaluation questions. At this point, only one group receives the intervention. Multiple measurements of progress toward outcomes are made in both groups. After some predetermined number of measurements, the second group receives the intervention, and both groups continue to be measured for progress toward stated outcomes. Thus, the first series of posttests will measure differences between the two groups, and subsequent ones will measure the maintenance of effects.

Quasi-experimental Designs

The hallmark of quasi-experimental designs is that random assignment is not used. When intact groups must be used in order to conduct the evaluation, a quasi-experimental design should be chosen. Evaluators should work to make sure that the experimental and comparison groups are as similar as possible and be prepared to describe how they are not similar. In general, one or more groups receive the new program that is being evaluated and one or more groups do not receive any program or receive the existing program. Multiple groups and/or multiple waves of measurement may be used.

Quasi-experimental Time Series

$$M^1\ M^2\ M^3\ M^4 \qquad X \qquad M^1\ M^2\ M^3\ M^4$$
$$M^1\ M^2\ M^3\ M^4 \qquad\qquad\ \ M^1\ M^2\ M^3\ M^4$$

Quasi-experimental time series design is the same as the experimental time series design except that intact groups are used and/or there is no random assignment.

Nonequivalent Control Group

$$M \qquad X \qquad M$$
$$M \qquad\qquad\ \ M$$

Pretests are conducted to see if the two (or more) groups are equivalent. Evaluators can randomly assign the intervention to either group, but there is no random assignment of participants.

Nonexperimental Designs

Preexperimental designs are often selected for portions of the process evaluation. They cannot address questions concerning whether the program, in particular, is producing its intended effects, but they can provide structure for gathering insight to answer questions about such areas as participant and staff experiences and satisfaction, and barriers to implementation.

One Shot Case Study

       X   M

Pretest and Posttest

    M   X   M

> **Checkpoint 9.2**
>
> Explain the major differences among experimental, quasi-experimental, and nonexperimental research designs.

Threats to Internal Validity

Internal validity is associated with the evaluators' confidence in being able to say that the program caused the intended outcomes. Creating a situation where this confidence level is high is an evaluation design issue and a data collection issue (Neutens & Rubinson, 2002). When high internal validity is sought, evaluators try to control influences on the potential program outcomes that are external from the program. The major ways to control threats to internal validity include the use of random assignment, random selection, and control or comparison groups.

    Box 9.1 contains an overview of the threats to internal validity as identified by Campbell and Stanley (1963) and Cook and Campbell (1979).

Threats to External Validity

External validity addresses the questions, to whom do the results of the evaluation apply? and who else would produce similar results with the program? External validity threats come from data collection methods and the processes of selecting participants. Box 9.2 contains an overview of the threats to external validity as identified by Campbell and Stanley (1963) and Cook and Campbell (1979).

> **Checkpoint 9.3**
>
> You are evaluating a new health education unit. Two of the things you are interested in learning is whether the new unit increases knowledge of the benefits of physical activity and whether it increases the physical activity levels of the students. You randomly assign intact physical education classes in your school to control or experimental groups.
>
> Although you found great success in an innovative "low back school" evaluation, you discover that most of the clients who dropped out were those with the most serious back problems.
>
> Identify the threats to internal and external validity in these two situations.

After a lot of hard work, the program is up and running. Dee and Jose have organized the needs assessment data and all program planning materials and have made them available to those who are interested in looking at the process and the resulting program. The program evaluation is mapped out and process evaluation activities have already begun. They plan to work to make the evaluation report data available in a variety of forms. Now, on to the next project!

Box 9.1   Threats to internal validity.

History

This threat involves events that are external to the evaluation study and occur during the course of the evaluation or result from a preexisting history in one group. These threats are often unpredictable, yet may cause a change not related to the program. The use of a control or comparison group and pretests will help control this threat.

Maturation

This threat involves events of change, where the change would occur anyway, that happen during the duration of the program and influence program outcomes, for example, getting smarter or stronger from normal growth and development. Evaluations that include children, adolescents, and older people over a length of time must be concerned with this threat. The use of a control or comparison group will help control this threat.

Testing

This threat involves the effects of testing upon subsequent results. Just experiencing pretest measures may affect posttest results separately from the effects of the program. Having sufficient time between pretest and posttest measurements will help control this threat. The use of control or comparison groups will show the impact of the program even if the testing effect is present.

Instrumentation

This threat comes from a change in measurement tools or measurement procedures from pretest to posttest, or a difference in tools and procedures between groups. This could include a change in survey instruments, the use of differential data collection administration procedures, or the use of different equipment to make the measurements. Minimizing this threat involves using the same measurement tools and procedures for all groups, at every measurement event, and for each outcome measured, as well as training those collecting the data.

Statistical regression

Statistical regression is the concept that scores tend to move toward the mean over time. This can be a problem when using scores on the ends of the range to assign participants to groups, as it can make it look like the program is having an effect when it is not. Evaluators need to make sure that groups come from the full range of scores or from the same end of the range.

Selection

This threat results from bias in the selection of participants for comparison groups. Selection threats are often a problem when using volunteers and intact groups. Random assignment can minimize this threat, and the threat can be identified and somewhat controlled through the use of pretests.

Box 9.1   Threats to internal validity. (Continued)

Experimental mortality

This threat involves the differential loss of participants from experimental and control or comparison groups. When it occurs, it creates nonequivalent groups at the posttest stage. Having large enough samples involved in the evaluation study helps to minimize this threat, as does providing incentives to remain in the study or program. Whenever possible, evaluators must get information about those who do not complete all of the measurements, so they can determine if the remaining groups are still equivalent.

Selection-maturation interaction

In this threat, experimental and control or comparison groups have different maturation levels and speeds. Evaluators must carefully select groups when using intact groups or volunteers. Pretests are important to confirm that the same levels exist in each of the groups.

Contamination

This threat is based on the idea that the evaluators treat groups differently because of prior knowledge about the groups. This differential treatment contributes to changes toward the outcome. Assigning people other than those in charge of the evaluation design or program delivery to the data collection process will help minimize this threat.

Diffusion or imitation of treatments

In this threat, the control or comparison group interacts with the experimental group, potentially affecting the ability to see differences in the groups at the posttest stage. Selecting equivalent groups that are physically distant (e.g., two different school districts or schools rather than two different classes in the same school) will minimize this threat.

Compensatory equalization of treatments

This threat occurs when the control group insists on receiving the intervention. Providing a delayed intervention will help with this threat.

Compensatory rivalry

This threat occurs when the control group sees itself as an underdog and thus works harder. Delayed intervention and not letting the control group know it is a control group will help with this threat.

Resentful demoralization of respondents receiving less desirable treatment

Resentment may affect the ability to measure the true outcome of the program. Thompson and McClintock suggest that evaluators must pay particular attention to history and maturation threats.*

*Thompson, N. J. & McClintock, H. O. (1998), *Demonstrating your program's worth: A primer on evaluation for programs to prevent unintentional injury.* Atlanta, GA: Centers for Disease Control and Prevention; National Center for Injury Prevention and Control.

Box 9.2   Threats to external validity.

Hawthorne effect

This threat results when singling out participants makes them act differently. Downplaying anything special about being involved in the evaluation will help minimize this threat.

Novelty and disruption effects

This threat exists when the program may be successful just because it is something new and different. Multiple posttests will help to identify if this was a problem.

Expectancy effect

This threat occurs when attitudes projected onto participants cause them to act differently. Facilitator and data collection training is important.

Social desirability

This threat occurs when respondents give evaluators and data collectors answers that they think will please, or that they think are the "right" answers even if it is not what they really think. Consider blind studies where appropriate.

Evaluators may want to consider blind studies for impact evaluations. In blind studies, participants do not know which group they are in (experimental or control). In double-blind studies, the type of groups participants are in is not known by participants or data collectors. In triple-blind studies, the type of group participants are in is not known to participants, data collectors, or researchers.

Summary

A program evaluation plan should include a combination of approaches that are designed to answer evaluation questions posed by the various stakeholders. Process evaluation should include a wide variety of approaches to most appropriately address its variety of questions. Quality impact and outcome evaluations, at the very least, require the use of experimental or quasi-experimental evaluation designs.

QUESTIONS

1. What are the key elements of the different evaluation approaches?
2. Why is it difficult for those evaluating health education and health promotion programs to use experimental designs? What do they "lose" by not being able to use experimental designs?

3. Why are nonexperimental designs often appropriate for process evaluation activities?

4. Describe, in your own words, the threats to internal validity. Give two examples.

5. Describe, in your own words, the threats to external validity. Give two examples.

EXERCISES

1. Locate and read the articles describing the evaluation of the Teenage Health Teaching Modules in the *Journal of School Health,* January 1991. Write a short paper describing the various components of the evaluation and the evaluation results.

2. Design an evaluation for a health-related program on your campus with which you are familiar.

REFERENCES

Campbell, D. T. & Stanley, J. C. (1963). *Experimental and quasi-experimental designs for research.* Boston: Houghton Mifflin.

Cook, T. D. & Campbell, D. T. (1979). *Quasi-experimentation: Design and analysis issues for field settings.* Chicago: Rand McNally.

Neutens, J. J. & Rubinson, L. (2002). Research techniques for the health sciences (3rd ed.). San Francisco: Benjamin Cummings.

Scriven, M. (1972). Pros and cons about goal-free evaluation. *Evaluation Comment, 3*(4), 1–7.

Springett, J. (2003). Issues in participatory evaluation. In Minkler, M. & Wallerstein, N. (eds.), *Community-based participatory research for health* (pp. 263–288). San Francisco: Jossey-Bass.

Stufflebeam, D. L. (2002). *The CIPP evaluation model checklist.* Retrieved August 15, 2003, from http://eval.cgu.edu.

Stufflebeam, D. L. (1973). Evaluation as enlightenment for decision-making. In Worthen, B. R. & Sanders, J. R. (eds.), *Educational evaluation: Theory and practice.* Belmont, CA: Wadsworth.

Thompson, N. J. & McClintock, H. O. (1998). *Demonstrating your program's worth: A primer on evaluation for programs to prevent unintentional injury.* Atlanta, GA: Centers for Disease Control and Prevention; National Center for Injury Prevention and Control.

Worthen, B. R. & Sanders, J. R. (1987). *Educational evaluation: Alternative approaches and practical guidelines.* New York: Longman.

1

Responsibility and Competency Areas Related to Needs Assessment, Program Planning, and Implementation

Note: Subcompetencies in bold are for the graduate level.

Responsibility I: Assessing Individual and Community Needs for Health Education

Competency A: Obtain Health-Related Data About Social and Cultural Environments and Growth and Development Factors, Needs, and Interests

Subcompetency

1. Select valid sources of information about health needs and interests.
2. Utilize computerized sources of health-related information.
3. Employ or develop appropriate data-gathering instruments.
4. Apply survey techniques to acquire health data.
5. **Conduct health-related needs assessments in communities.**

Competency B: Distinguish Between Behaviors That Foster and Those That Hinder Well-Being

Subcompetency

1. Investigate physical, social, emotional, and intellectual factors influencing health behaviors.
2. Identify behaviors that tend to promote or compromise health.
3. Recognize the role of learning and affective experiences in shaping patterns of health behavior.
4. **Analyze social, cultural, economic, and political factors that influence health behavior.**

Competency C: Infer Needs for Health Education on the Basis of Obtained Data

Subcompetency

1. Analyze needs assessment data.

2. Determine priority areas of need for health education.

Competency D: Determine Factors That Influence Learning and Development

Subcompetency

1. Assess individual learning styles.

2. Assess individual literacy.

3. Assess the learning environment.

Responsibility II: Planning Effective Health Education Programs

Competency A: Recruit Community Organizations, Resource People, and Potential Participants for Support and Assistance in Program Planning

Subcompetency

1. Communicate the need for the program to those who will be involved.

2. Obtain commitments from personnel and decision-makers who will be involved in the program.

3. Seek ideas and opinions of those who will affect or be affected by the program.

4. Incorporate feasible ideas and recommendations into the planning process.

5. Apply principles of community organization in planning programs.

Competency B: Develop a Logical Scope and Sequence Plan for a Health Education Program

Subcompetency

1. Determine the range of health information requisite to a given program of instruction.

2. Organize the subject areas comprising the scope of a program in logical sequence.

3. Review philosophical and theory-based foundations in planning health education programs.

4. Analyze the process for integrating health education as part of a broader health care or education program.

5. Develop a theory-based framework for health education programs.

Competency C: Formulate Appropriate and Measurable Program Objectives
Subcompetency

1. Infer educational objectives that facilitate the achievement of specified competencies.
2. Develop a framework of broadly stated, operational objectives relevant to a proposed health education program.

Competency D: Design Educational Programs That Are Consistent with Specified Program Objectives
Subcompetency

1. Match proposed learning activities with those implicit in the stated objectives.
2. Formulate a wide variety of alternative educational methods.
3. Select strategies that are best suited to the implementation of educational objectives in a given setting.
4. Plan a sequence of learning opportunities, building upon and reinforcing mastery of preceding objectives.
5. Select appropriate theory-based strategies in health program planning.
6. Plan training and instructional programs for health professionals.

Competency E: Develop Health Education Programs Using Social Marketing Principles
Subcompetency

1. Identify populations for health education programs.
2. Involve participants in planning health education programs.
3. Design a marketing plan to promote health education.

Responsibility III: Implementing Health Education Programs

Competency A: Exhibit Competency in Carrying Out Planned Educational Programs
Subcompetency

1. Employ a wide range of educational methods and techniques.
2. Apply individual or group process methods as appropriate to the given learning situations.
3. Utilize instructional equipment and other instructional media effectively.

4. Select methods that best facilitate the practice of program objectives.

5. Assess, select, and apply technologies that will contribute to program objectives.

6. Develop, demonstrate, and model implementation strategies.

7. Deliver an educational program for health professionals.

8. Use community organization principles to guide and facilitate community development.

Competency B: Infer Enabling Objectives as Needed to Implement Instructional Programs in Specified Settings

Subcompetency

1. Pretest learners to ascertain present abilities and knowledge relative to proposed program objectives.

2. Develop subordinate measurable objectives as needed for instruction.

Competency C: Select Methods and Media Best Suited to Implement Program Plans for Specific Learners

Subcompetency

1. Analyze learner characteristics, legal aspects, feasibility, and other considerations that influence choices among methods.

2. Evaluate the efficacy of alternative methods and techniques that are capable of facilitating program objectives.

3. Determine the availability of information, personnel, time, and equipment needed to implement the program for a given audience.

4. Critically analyze technologies, methods, and media for their acceptability to diverse groups.

5. Apply theoretical and conceptual models from health education and related disciplines to improve program delivery.

Competency D: Monitor Educational Programs and Adjust Objectives and Activities as Necessary

Subcompetency

1. Compare actual program activities with their stated objectives.

2. Assess the relevance of existing program objectives to current needs.

3. Revise program activities and objectives as necessitated by changes in learner needs.

4. Appraise applicability of resources and materials to given educational objectives.

Responsibility IV: Evaluating the Effectiveness of Health Education Programs

Competency A: Develop Plans to Assess the Achievement of Program Objectives

Subcompetency

1. Determine standards of performance to be applied as criteria for effectiveness.
2. Establish a realistic scope of evaluation efforts.
3. Develop an inventory of existing valid and reliable tests and survey instruments.
4. Select appropriate methods for evaluating program effectiveness.
5. Identify existing sources of health-related databases.
6. Evaluate existing data-gathering instruments and processes.
7. Select appropriate qualitative and/or quantitative evaluation designs.
8. Develop valid and reliable evaluation instruments.

Competency B: Carry Out Evaluation Plans

Subcompetency

1. Facilitate the administration of tests and activities specified in the plan.
2. Utilize data collection methods that are appropriate to the objectives.
3. Analyze the resulting evaluation data.
4. Implement the appropriate qualitative and quantitative evaluation techniques.
5. Apply evaluation technology as appropriate.

Competency C: Interpret the Results of the Program Evaluation

Subcompetency

1. Apply criteria of effectiveness to the obtained results of a program.
2. Translate the evaluation results into terms easily understood by others.
3. Report the effectiveness of educational programs in achieving proposed objectives.
4. Implement strategies to analyze data from evaluation assessments.
5. Compare evaluation results to other findings.
6. Make recommendations based on the evaluation results.

Competency D: Evaluating the Effectiveness of Health Education Programs

Subcompetency

1. Explore possible explanations for important evaluation findings.
2. Recommend strategies for implementing the results of the evaluation.
3. Apply findings to refine and maintain programs.
4. Use evaluation findings in policy analysis and development.

Source: Capwell, E. (1997). Health education graduate standards: Expansion of the framework. *Health Education and Behavior,* 24(2), 137–150.

2

Social and Health Assessment Example: Cortland Counts

The Seven Valleys Health Coalition of Cortland County, NY, in cooperation with the county health department, the local hospital, the local state university, and the local United Way conducted an "Assessment of Health and Well Being." The assessment provided a set of indicators in five areas: health and safety; social cohesion, culture, and recreation; employment, economy, and welfare; housing and environment; and positive development through life stages. The assessment was the first part of a three-stage process in setting health and well-being priorities and was conducted by a community assessment team (CAT). Examples of data collected in each of the five areas are as follows:

1. Social cohesion: engagement in volunteer activities, percentage of registered voters voting, and attendance at cultural events

2. Employment, economy, and welfare: per capita personal income, unemployment rates, and percentage of children receiving public assistance

3. Housing and environment: measurement of water quality, senior housing units, recycling, and substandard housing

4. Positive development through the life stages: numbers of day care slots, high school dropouts, high school graduates enrolled in higher education, children in foster care, and persons (aged 10 to 15 years) in need of supervision (PINS)

5. Health and safety: percentage of low birth weight babies; teen pregnancy rates; and prevalence and mortality rates for a variety of cancers, diseases of the heart, hepatitis B, unintentional injuries, violent crime, and a variety of respiratory problems

The health and well-being assessment findings were shared with the community in a number of different ways during the second stage of the process (including report cards, articles in the local newspaper, and community forums). Community feedback was further encouraged by asking community members to telephone, e-mail, or write the CAT.

The third stage entailed setting health and well-being priorities for the county based on the assessment and the feedback from the community on the data from the assessment. A Blue Ribbon Committee was convened, which consisted of elected officials; media representatives; health, mental health, and medical professionals; labor and business leaders; drug and alcohol prevention, accessibility, and cultural advocates; youth and senior representatives; and educators to assist in priority setting. The Blue Ribbon Committee identified economic development, health, youth, and county administrative priorities. The priorities were disseminated through an updated community report card for more feedback. Once slight adjustments were made based on community feedback, several new work groups were formed to further investigate what needed to be done in the community to address the health and well-being priorities. One of these work groups, the Task Force for Health Promotion, is involved, at this writing, in primary and secondary data collection in order to identify the behavioral and environmental factors contributing to the health priorities.

Source: The Seven Valleys Health Coalition (2001). *Cortland counts: An assessment of health and well being in Cortland County.* Cortland, NY: The Seven Valleys Health Coalition.

3

Sample Moderator Script for a Focus Group Interview

Hello, my name is _____ and this is _____.
We are from _____ and are interested in
finding out what middle school students, like yourselves, think about health
and health education. Your school is putting together a new health education
class and has asked us to find out what the students think. I will be asking the
group some questions, and _____ will be taking notes so we
do not miss some of the important things you have to say. This discussion, as
you know, is being audiotaped so that, later on, I can fill in our notes to make
sure that we really got what you need.

What you say here today is confidential, no one will know what you,
specifically, had to say. The only people who will hear it are _____,
myself, and the person who will type up the audiotapes. After what was said
on the tapes has been written down, the tapes will be erased. Later on, I will
write a report describing the major points we all heard today so that your
school can put together a class that students, such as yourselves, will find in-
teresting and useful. You were all picked by numbers, so I do not know who
any of you are. You have all put first names on your name tags but, as explained, you could have picked any name, not necessarily yours!

Let's get started.

1. If you could choose another name for yourself, what would it be?
   During this group discussion this will be your name. (After each has
   given a name, have them write it down on the name tags provided.)

2. What do you like to do in your free time?

3. Do you have health education class in middle school? What do you think
   people your age need to learn in health education? (Probe: How come?)

177

4. Sometimes, young people do things that may be considered risky, or they take chances. How many of your friends and classmates do things that you think are risky or dangerous?

5. What kinds of things do they do that you think are risky and dangerous to their health? (Probe: Why do you think these things are risky or dangerous to their health?)

6. What kinds of things do your four closest friends do that you think are risky or dangerous to their health?

7. What kinds of activities do you do that may be considered risky or dangerous by your four closest friends? (Probe: Why do you think these things may be risky or dangerous?)

8. Do you have any questions for us? What are they?

action: A stage of the Transtheoretical Model. Those who have recently (within the past 6 months) put health-compromising behavior change plans into place are in this stage.

activities: The specific components or strategies of the intervention that are developed to help the target population achieve the program objectives and ultimately the program goal. Activity examples include a radio-based public service announcement, a workshop on increasing physical activity levels, a brochure on the prevention of HIV, or other means to deliver a message or create the desired change.

adversary-oriented: An evaluation approach that actively seeks to elicit opposing viewpoints in an effort to make the evaluation as unbiased as possible. It includes discussion and presentation of both the strengths and weaknesses of the program.

APEXPH: Assessment Protocol for Excellence in Public Health; which is designed to provide guidance for local health departments in conducting community and organizational self-assessments, planning improvements, evaluations, and reassessments.

behavioral capability: Potential based on the concept that knowledge plus skills influence behavior. It is part of the Social Cognitive Theory.

behavioral intent: A person expects to take a specific action sometime in the future.

CIPP Model: A management-oriented evaluation approach that includes process, impact, effectiveness, sustainability, transportability, and meta-evaluation components. The model was developed by Stufflebeam.

coalition: A group of groups working together toward achieving common goals and objectives.

community: A group of people who have common characteristics, such as location, ethnicity, age, or occupation.

community capacity: The strengths and skills of individuals and groups within a community that, now and in the future, may contribute to the quality of life of the entire community.

consumer-oriented: An evaluation approach that includes independent evaluations of products and programs based on a predetermined set of criteria. This approach is usually taken in order to provide information to those considering the use or purchase of products or programs.

contamination: A threat to internal validity in which researchers or evaluators treat experimental and comparison or control groups differently because of prior knowledge about the groups, limiting the evaluator's ability to conclude that the program influenced measured outcomes.

contemplation: A stage of the Transtheoretical Model characterized by one's recognition that there may be a problem with engaging in a particular health-compromising behavior and one's intention to change it within 6 months.

cultural appropriateness: The goal of developing interventions that will meet the needs of the target population with an understanding of the cultural experiences and influences that shape their behaviors and environment.

decision/determination: A stage of the Transtheoretical Model characterized by one's recognition that there may be a problem with engaging in a particular health-compromising behavior. Individuals in this stage intend to change the behavior within 30 days, have taken some steps toward change, or have made plans to change.

efficiency evaluation: A cost-benefit evaluation.

enabling factor: A factor, often environmental in nature, that allows a behavior to begin or to continue or allows an institution to act. It also refers to the availability, accessibility, and cost of services and goods needed to engage in a behavior or to sustain an environmental factor. It may also refer to the new skills that individuals communities, or organizations need before a behavior can be carried out or an environmental factor can be changed. It is part of phase four of the Precede–Proceed model.

evidence-based or science-based: Generally refers to a program or intervention with a theoretical foundation that has been shown to be effective based on scientific evidence.

expectancy effect: A threat to external validity in which attitudes that are projected onto participants by facilitators or data collectors cause participants to act differently than they normally would. This limits the evaluator's ability to generalize the results of the evaluation.

expectation: What one thinks will happen. It is one of the facets of Social Cognitive Theory, which asserts that one may or may not act, based on what one thinks will happen as a result of engaging in a behavior.

experimental design: A research design based on the random assignment of participants into one or more groups and the measurement of all groups. This is the strongest design.

experimental mortality: A threat to internal validity in which experimental and control or comparison groups lose different types of participants in different amounts during the course of a study or evaluation. This creates groups at the posttest stage that are no longer equivalent to each other, limiting the evaluator's ability to conclude that the program influenced measured outcomes.

expertise-oriented: An evaluation approach in which professional experts provide feedback and judgement on products or programs.

external validity: The ability to apply the results of an experiment or evaluation beyond that particular situation. In program evaluation, it points to those to whom the results apply, and suggests who else may get similar results with the program.

formative evaluation: Evaluation conducted for the purpose of getting information to be used to improve a program. It may occur during program planning or implementation.

goals: Statements that provide specific long-term direction for a program, which are used to present the overall intent or desired program outcome.

Hawthorne effect: A threat to external validity in which subjects in a study or participants in an evaluation act differently than they normally would just because they are involved in the study or evaluation. This limits the evaluator's ability to generalize the results of the evaluation.

health education: Any combination of planned learning experiences based on sound theories that provide individuals, groups, and communities the opportunity to acquire information and the skills needed to make quality health decisions.*

health promotion: Any planned combination of educational, political, regulatory, and organizational supports for actions and conditions of living conducive to health in individuals, groups, or communities.†

history: A threat to internal validity in which events external to the evaluation study occur during the course of the evaluation or a preexisting history in one group is found that would limit the evaluator's ability to conclude that the program influenced measured outcomes.

impact evaluation: A measurement of the extent to which a program has caused the intended short-term changes in the target population.

incidence: A reference to new occurrences of illnesses or conditions in a population during a given time frame.

---

*Gold, R. S. & Miner, K. R. (2002). Report of the 2000 Joint Committee on Health Education and Promotion Terminology. *Journal of School Health*, 72(1), 3–7.

*Green, L. W. & Kreuter, M. W. (1999). *Health promotion planning: An educational and ecological approach* (3rd ed.). Mountain View, CA: Mayfield.

instrumentation: A threat to internal validity in which there is a change in measurement tools or measurement procedures from pretest to posttest or a difference in tools and procedures between groups that would limit the evaluator's ability to conclude that the program influenced measured outcomes.

internal validity: The level of control of all outside influences, except those that are being looked at, in an experiment or an evaluation. It is associated with the evaluators' confidence in being able to say that the program caused the intended outcomes.

intervention: The means by which the program planners attempt to achieve the stated outcomes or goal.

key informant: A person in the community or target group or a person working with the community or target group who has access to information about the group.

maintenance: A stage of the Transtheoretical Model characterized by one's continuation of the health-enhancing action for more than 6 months.

management-oriented: An evaluation approach conducted in order to assist administrators in making decisions about the program. It is focused on questions generated by program managers and stakeholders.

maturation: A threat to internal validity in which events of change, where the change would occur anyway, happen during the duration of the program that would limit the evaluator's ability to conclude that the program influenced measured outcomes.

method: The theory-based technique used to influence behavior or the environment and, ultimately, to create the change needed to achieve the program goal or outcomes. This framework then results in the development of the specific strategies or activities.

mission statement: A broad statement used to present the idea of the long-term impact of the program and is sometimes referred to as the statement of purpose.

model: A simplistic representation of a complex problem or concept.

morbidity: The occurrence of illness or conditions in a population.

mortality: The occurrence of death caused by illness and conditions in a population.

multiple intelligences: The concept that individuals have different learning styles and abilities, which was initially articulated through the work of Dr. Howard Gardner.

naturalistic-oriented: An evaluation approach that provides a broad description of the program and its outcomes from multiple perspectives using a variety of types of data. The perspectives of the participants are most important.

needs assessment: The systematic collection of information to help identify the health problems in the target population, the antecedents to these problems, and programming needs and ideas. It is also a necessary part of program planning and implementation, and it serves as the beginning of program evaluation.

novelty and disruption effect: A threat to external validity in which evaluation participants respond to the fact that the program being evaluated is something new and different, rather than to the program itself. This limits the evaluator's ability to generalize the results of the evaluation.

objectives: A specific statement of short-term application directed toward achieving the program goal, usually written in measurable terms and including references to program activities or strategies.

objectives-oriented: An evaluation approach focused on program outcomes, which may be predetermined or unintended actual outcomes.

observational learning: Beliefs that arise from watching others similar to oneself or from seeing physical results.

outcome evaluation: A measurement of the extent to which a program has caused the intended long-term changes in the target population.

PATCH: Planned Approach to Community Health, which is a model that provides a general structure for the needs assessment, program planning, and evaluation process that emphasizes community involvement and linkages among a variety of agencies and services associated with the community.

perceived barriers: One's own assessment of the downside or impediments to engaging in a recommended health-related behavior or action. These represent a key construct of the Health Belief Model.

perceived benefits: One's own assessment of the benefits of engaging in a recommended health-related behavior or action. These represent a key construct of the Health Belief Model.

perceived severity: One's own assessment of the seriousness of a health problem. It answers the question, how high or serious are the costs (physical, emotional, and economic) of having this health problem? This represents a key construct of the Health Belief Model.

perceived susceptibility: One's own assessment of the level of risk of experiencing a health problem. It answers the question, how likely am I to get "X"? This represents a key construct of the Health Belief Model.

personal determinates: Personal factors that have a strong influence on explaining why individuals engage in a specific behavior or not. Personal determinates include such variables as prior knowledge, attitudes, social influences, and skills.

philosophy: A statement that helps to identify the beliefs or values that form the basis of a program and further define its mission.

planning committee: A panel or committee of selected individuals convened to plan an intervention or program.

potential consumer: The individuals or target group that the program was designed to serve.

potential program provider: Individuals or agencies identified to give or implement the strategies or activities of the program to the target population.

Precede–Proceed: A health planning model. Acronym stands for Predisposing, Reinforcing, and Enabling Constructs in Educational/ecological Diagnosis and Evaluation-Policy, Regulatory, and Organizational Constructs in Educational and Environmental Development.

precontemplation: A stage of the Transtheoretical Model in which one is unaware that one's engagement in a particular health-compromising behavior may be a problem and has no thoughts about changing the behavior.

predisposing factors: Knowledge, attitudes, beliefs, values, or self-efficacy that exist prior to the engagement in a health-related behavior. These exist "inside a person's head." They are part of phase four of the Precede–Proceed model.

prevalence: A reference to the total number of occurrences of an illness or condition in a population during a given time frame.

primary data: Information collected directly from people.

process evaluation: An evaluation conducted in order to explain why a program may or may not have been effective. This often includes implementation monitoring, the measurement of progress toward goals and objectives; the assessment of satisfaction levels, staff performance reviews, and resource reviews.

program desired outcome: The goal that the program or intervention was designed to achieve, which could potentially differ from the actual goal or the end results of the intervention.

program ownership: The establishment of connections with potential program providers and consumers to ensure that communication occurs and a sense of belonging develops with regard to an intervention or program that is being planned.

programs that work: Programs and interventions that have been identified by the professional literature to have the potential to achieve the desired program objectives or outcomes.

qualitative: Descriptive, nonnumerical, and contextual. Qualitative data are often words or pictures.

quality of life: The sense of individuals and groups of having their needs met and not having barriers to opportunities to become happy and fulfilled.

quantitative: Empirical and numerical. Quantitative data can undergo mathematical and statistical operations.

quasi-experimental design: A research design that compares two or more groups, but does not require random assignment. This design is weaker than experimental designs, but is conducive to use in the "real world."

reciprocal determinism: An underlying concept of the Social Cognitive Theory that asserts that behavior, environment, and people are all interrelated.

reinforcement: Physical, social, emotional or other responses to behavior that increase or decrease the likelihood of a behavior continuing or being repeated.

reinforcing factors: Physical, social, and emotional responses of other people or institutions that reward the continued engagement in a behavior. These are part of phase four of the Precede–Proceed model.

resources: Time, money, and people.

sampling: Selecting a representative subset of an entire population.

secondary data: Information collected by someone else.

selection: A threat to internal validity in which there is a bias in the selection of participants for comparison groups. This limits the evaluator's ability to conclude that the program influenced measured outcomes.

self-efficacy: Having or perceiving the confidence or ability to engage in a skill or behavior. This is generally considered when trying to facilitate a health-enhancing behavior in a specific target population.

social desirability: A threat to external validity in which research or evaluation participants respond to data collectors in a way that they think will please or with what they think are the "right" answers even if they are not their "real" answers. This limits the evaluator's ability to generalize the results of the evaluation.

strategies: See activities.

summative evaluation: An evaluation conducted for the purpose of determining whether a program worked.

tailoring: Shaping a program or intervention to meet the needs of the target group. This is often done to make the program more relevant and effective, based on the characteristics of the target population that were identified during the initial planning phases.

testing: A threat to internal validity in which the effects of prior testing upon subsequent results limit the evaluator's ability to conclude that the program influenced measured outcomes.

theory: A way to understand a problem. This can sometimes offer a way to predict or control a problem.

INDEX